Qigong for Health

QIGONG for HEALTH

*Chinese Traditional Exercises
for Cure and Prevention*

by Masaru Takahashi
and Stephen Brown

Japan Publications, Inc.

Note to the reader: The information contained in this book is not intended to be used in the diagnosis, prescription, or treatment of disease or any health disorder whatsoever. Nor is this information intended to replace competent medical care. This book is a compendium of information which may be used as an adjunct to a rational and responsible health care plan.

Published by JAPAN PUBLICATIONS, INC., Tokyo and New York

Distributors:
UNITED STATES: *Kodansha International/USA, Ltd., through Farrar, Straus & Giroux, 19 Union Square West, New York, 1003.* CANADA: *Fitzhenry & Whiteside Ltd., 195 Allstate Parkway, Markham, Ontario, L3R 4T8.* BRITISH ISLES AND EUROPEAN CONTINENT: *Premier Book Marketing Ltd., 1 Gower Street, London WC1E 6HA.* AUSTRALIA AND NEW ZEALAND: *Bookwise International, 54 Critenden Road, Findon, South Australia 5007.* THE FAR EAST AND JAPAN: *Japan Publications Trading Co., Ltd., 1-2-1, Sarugaku-cho, Chiyoda-ku, Tokyo 101.*

First edition: March 1986
Second printing: February 1991

LCCC No. 85–080718
ISBN 0–87040–701–5

Printed in U.S.A.

Foreword

This book came into being by the timely meeting of two acupuncturists, one Oriental and other Westerner, with a deep interest in Qigong. The Oriental acupuncturist is myself, and the Western acupuncturist is Stephen Brown.

I have studied various Japanese martial arts since my youth and also have practiced Tai Chi Quan for many years. Through my study and practice of martial arts, I reached the conclusion that the basic foundation for martial arts in Japan and China is one and the same as that of Oriental medicine. The emphasis on Ki (Qi in Chinese), which is best understood as vital energy, is the same in martial arts and Oriental medicine. Also, the same vital points taught in martial arts are used for treatment in acupuncture. This realization compelled me to enter the field of acupuncture more than ten years ago.

Techniques for "nurturing" or developing Ki are of primary importance not only in Oriental medicine but in martial arts as well. These techniques for developing Ki generally take the form of breathing and mental concentration exercises practiced in special postures. Traditionally, in many schools of martial arts, such techniques for developing Ki were kept a closely guarded secret. Practices of this nature, for strengthening Ki and invigorating the spirit, actually existed in China well before acupuncture was developed in its present form. These practices originating in ancient China were known as Do-In (Daoyin in Chinese). In China today, the general term Qigong is used to describe all such practices for developing Ki.

When I learned that this valuable tradition was still being preserved and developed in China today, I decided that this was something I must study along with martial arts and acupuncture. It soon became quite clear to me from my study of Chinese literature on the subject that there were a multitude of different styles and schools in Qigong. Among all the methods, the method of Qigong developed by Dr. Liu Gui-zhen, Director of the Beidaihe Qigong Therapy Institute in the Hebei Province, stood out as being the most systematic, scientific, and widely accepted approach. Once I became convinced that the methods of Dr. Liu were the most reliable approach to Qigong, I began to practice Inner Regulation Qigong, Vitalizing Qigong, and Preventive Qigong by closely following his book *Qigong Liaofa Shijian* (Practical Qigong Therapy). More than ten years after that I was finally able to fulfill my long time wish to study at the Beidaihe Qigong Therapy Institute. There, under the guidance of Dr. Liu's associates, I was able to confirm the validity of my own practice up until that time and I was satisfied to learn that all my years of self-study had not been in vain.

In this way I gained strong confidence in Dr. Liu's approach to Qigong as being invaluable, not only for sick people, but for all those who wished to increase their health and well-being. After returning to Japan, I began writing a serial feature on Qigong for a martial arts magazine. Stephen Brown contacted me not too long after that, and upon meeting him, I learned that he had lived in Japan many years and was, like myself, an acupuncturist. In addition to being fluent in Japanese, he also knew Chinese and was very knowledgable about Qigong and Oriental medicine. Further, I was surprised and delighted to learn that Mr. Brown, in all his study, had reached essentially the same conclusion as myself. We concurred that, among all the varieties of Qigong, the methods systematized by Dr. Liu Gui-zhen are the most widely used and reliable.

In our very first meeting we agreed that it would be a most worthwhile project to make this valuable knowledge available to Western readers. Therefore we began working together to compile this book about Dr. Liu's approach to Qigong. Through the process of writing this book we were able to draw on each other's experience and add to our knowledge of Qigong and Oriental medicine. This book was therefore the result of excellent teamwork between two practitioners, one Oriental and one Westerner.

It should be noted, however, that the basic framework of this book consists of the Qigong exercises systematized by Dr. Liu Gui-zhen. Many of the practical details were supplemented based on the experience of Mr. Brown and myself.

Mr. Brown has done an excellent job of organizing and presenting this material in a form acceptable to a Western readership. As to the contents of this book, however, I am largely accountable. The introduction to Qigong at the very beginning of this book is my description of Qigong. Also, the notes on acupuncture treatments in the final part of this book on treatment of diseases are based on my own clinical experience. This book is probably the first book in the West to introduce the Eight Basic Tai Chi Forms. I decided to include these Tai Chi exercises because they are the simplest and most direct approach to Tai Chi that allow a beginner to get a taste for the profound power behind this hard-to-master practice.

Since I started practicing Qigong on my own by studying the Chinese texts available, I am well aware of the importance of the format in these books. I think it is worthwhile to point out four special features of this book which distinguish it from other Qigong books: First is a wealth of step by step photographic detail, second is advice on Qigong practice for various diseases, third is a simplified version of Tai Chi for self-learning, and fourth is specific advice on acupuncture treatments. The first three of these features can be readily appreciated and put to use by the general public. The last feature, however, is more for the benefit of those with some background in Oriental medicine. I would have liked to go into greater depth in this respect since Qigong is so deeply connected in its theory and practice with Oriental medicine. I only regret that this was beyond the scope of this book.

In conclusion, I would like to express my deep gratitude to Dr. Chang Tian-ge and Dr. Tian Hong-ji at the Beidaihe Qigong Therapy Institute who unsparingly gave me their instruction and advice during my period of study at the institute. Also we are deeply indebted to Iwao Yoshizaki, the president of Japan Publications, Inc., for his enthusiastic support.

MASARU TAKAHASHI

Contents

8

Chapter 1

An Introduction to Qigong

What is Qigong?

Qigong (pronounced Cheekung) is a Chinese term applied to all forms of exercise which work with one's Qi. According to Oriental medicine Qi [気], in its wide sense, is everything from the air we breathe to the vital energy which animates our bodies. Gong [功] means to work with or to train. Thus Qigong could be best understood simply as breath training, although it is a great deal more than that. Qi, along with its close relationship to the function of respiration, provides resistance against disease, facilitates adaptation to one's environment, and supplies the energy necessary for the continual process of regeneration taking place within our bodies. So naturally, having an abundance of Qi yields good health, and this is the most essential factor in preventing illness. Also this is why some form of "Qi training" (breathing exercise) is regarded as being of primary importance in Oriental medicine, which includes acupuncture and herbology. Qigong is used as a general term to cover all types of training which develop one's Qi or energetic capacity, and most often this takes the form of breath training for developing one's "source Qi," which in turn strengthens the body. The term Qigong is commonly used to imply exercises which work particularly to strengthen the internal organs, in contrast to those which build muscles, but the more precise term for this type of Qigong is Neigong [内功] (internal training). There are countless styles and techniques of Qigong which have been developed through China's long history, and Tai Chi Quan counts among these. All types of Qigong can be divided into either Jinggong [静功] (passive training), where the body remains motionless, or Donggong [動功] (active training), where the body is moved. Jinggong can be done while standing, sitting, or lying down. Donggong covers all types of Qigong where the body is moved, so it ranges from relatively nonstrenuous exercises such as Yijinjing [易筋経], a series of twelve stationary exercises said to have originated with Bodhi Dharma, to the lightning action of Chinese martial arts such as Kungfu. The main "active training" Qigong exercise introduced in this book is called Stepping Qigong and was developed by Dr. Liu Gui-zhen, the foremost authority on Qigong therapy in mainland China.

The one word Qigong, therefore, encompasses a broad range of exercise systems for developing one's Qi, but all these methods have three basic elements or principles in common. These principles are Diaoshen [調身], which means to adjust or prepare posture, Diaoxi [調息] (pronounced Diaoshi), which means to adjust or regulate breath, and Diaoxin [調心] (pronounced Diaoshin), which means to adjust or calm

Categories of Qigong

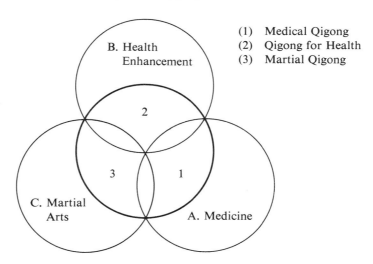

(1) Medical Qigong
(2) Qigong for Health
(3) Martial Qigong

B. Health Enhancement

2

3   1

C. Martial Arts

A. Medicine

the mind. Each method of Qigong has its special features, and each method emphasizes slightly different aspects, but the objectives of all types of Qigong can be categorized into three kinds. These are medical Qigong, Qigong for health, and martial Qigong. Refer to the diagram above. The thick circle in the center represents the entire scope of Qigong; circle A is the field of medicine, circle B is activity done to build and maintain health, and circle C is martial arts.

Medical Qigong (the portion of circle A which lies within the Qigong circle) is Qigong performed as therapy for chronic diseases and is also referred to as Qigong Exercise Therapy. This category also includes Qigong treatments performed by a Qigong master, where energy is projected to special points on the patient's body to produce an anesthetic effect as well as to have a curative effect. Therefore, medical Qigong also includes both the active and passive approaches.

Qigong for health (the portion of circle B which lies within the Qigong circle) is Qigong performed on a regular basis to stay healthy and prevent illness. In Oriental medicine, best known as Chinese acupuncture and herbology, great emphasis is placed on treating a disease in its incipient stages before it produces definite physical symptoms. This is the primary purpose of various Do-In and Tai-Chi exercises—to cure diseases before they become manifest. Qigong for health is performed for the exact same reason.

Martial Qigong (the portion of circle C which lies within the Qigong circle) is the groundwork for training in the martial arts, and its main purpose is to strengthen muscles and build endurance. Ma-Bu (horse stance), one of the basic postures in Chinese martial arts, is also considered to be a type of Qigong exercise. There are other more rigorous training regimens such as "Iron Fist Qigong," where the fist is hardened by repeatedly striking hard objects, and "Battering Qigong," where one's body is struck and beaten over and over to toughen it up against blows.

Another broad classification for Qigong is the hard and soft styles. Qigong exercises for martial arts training are generally referred to as "Hard Qigong," while all those Qigong exercises for building and nurturing health are called "Soft Qigong." The various feats of physical endurance demonstrated by Qigong masters all over China are all demonstrations of "Hard Qigong." The Qigong exercises which are now gaining worldwide attention as a cure for cancer and other serious illnesses are "Soft Qigong." Qigong masters projecting energy into patients during surgery for the purpose of anesthesia is also classified as "Soft Qigong."

In this way, while Qigong is just a simple word which means "breath training," it covers a very broad scope of exercises and practices from ancient Taoist mysticism to applications for anesthesia in operating rooms of modern hospitals. The most common form of Qigong, the type practiced most widely among the Chinese people today, is those exercises for restoring and maintaining health, which belong to the category of Soft Qigong. This is the Qigong for building health and vitality, which is the subject of this book.

Qigong as Therapy

How Qigong Cures Disease

In China Qigong is being applied in the field of medicine for the treatment of chronic diseases. According to recent studies conducted in China, Qigong therapy has been proven effective for the treatment of a great number of diseases including neurosis, hypertension, ulcers, gastroptosis, and chronic constipation. Naturally, since it has been found to be so effective, Qigong is being used as therapy for a wide variety of diseases, aside from being widely practiced by the Chinese public as a means of staying in excellent health.

It is said that there are three basic therapeutic principles behind the effectiveness of Qigong. These are the restoration of vitality, the storage of physical energy, and the massaging action on the visceral organs.

More specifically, the restoration of vitality means to replenish the depleted energy reserves of the body through proper rest and recuperation of physical systems, as well as to gradually increase weakened resistance by restoring normal organic function. According to physiological studies conducted in China, during the deeply relaxed state achieved by the practice of Qigong, the excitation of the cerebral cortex is suppressed by internal inhibition. Overexcitation and fatigue of the cerebral cortex can be relieved by remaining in such a calm and quiet state for extended periods, and this restores the brain to its normal calm and alert condition.

In other words, those parts of the brain which are difficult to calm down and remain hyperactive are quieted by internal control to create conditions in the central nervous system more conducive to the regeneration of vitality and the recovery of health. The effectiveness of Qigong against nervous disorders such as neurosis, ulcers, and hypertension is thought to be due to this therapeutic principle since the cause and development of these three diseases are intimately related to the psychological condition of the patient.

The second therapeutic principle of storing physical energy is essential to the practice of Qigong. In physiological studies, when Qigong is being practiced, the body has been shown to enter into an "energy storing phase." This refers to a state of parasympathetic tonus seen in deep relaxation or sleep, where oxygen consumption is reduced by some 30 percent and the metabolic rate decreases about 20 percent. Remaining in this "energy storing phase" for a long period while still in a waking state stops the loss of energy and facilitates the storage of fresh energy supplies obtained by the body. Boosting one's energy level in this way is one of the main reasons that Qigong is effective for people with chronic and debilitative conditions, as well as for those with a weak physical constitution.

The third therapeutic factor of Qigong is the effect of massaging the organs in the abdominal cavity. The mechanical action of deep abdominal breathing serves to massage and stimulate the activity of internal organs. The breathing techniques practiced in Qigong have a remarkable massaging effect on the vital organs. In this special breathing, the range of movement in the diaphragm becomes three to four times greater than that during normal breathing. This movement of the diaphragm rhythmically massages the visceral organs to stimulate the function of the stomach and intestines and thereby improves digestion and absorption. This massaging action is also effective in reducing the congestion of blood in the lower abdomen. It is common for people to experience an improvement in their appetite after practicing Qigong, and it becomes easier to gain weight in a healthy way because of the greater efficiency of the digestive system resulting from the massaging action of deep abdominal breathing. This is the reason Qigong is so often effective in curing gastroptosis and chronic constipation.

How Qigong Can Cure Cancer

In the decade since the Cultural Revolution in China, a considerable number of articles and publications on Qigong have been published. Most of the literature on Qigong published in the 1970s points out the effectiveness of Qigong in treating chronic diseases as well as its benefits in terms of maintaining one's general health. Most of these publications introduce a few simple Qigong exercises that can be practiced by the reader. After 1980, however, numerous articles and books began to appear on Qigong in China focusing on "New Qigong," which is effective against cancer. Various Qigong masters and specialists in the field have now published case histories of successful cancer treatments using Qigong. Below are two typical examples of reports concerning cancer cures from Chinese publications:

> "In one department of a medical research institute, a Qigong master over sixty years of age projected energy to major acupuncture points on the head (Baihui, Taiyang, and Yintang) of a patient with cancer of the pharynx. This patient

was also given instructions on how to practice Qigong on his own. When tested six months later, the tumor in the nasal part of the pharynx had largely disappeared."

"In recent years, a group of cancer patients performed Qigong exercises under the guidance of a Qigong expert, in addition to receiving standard Western and Eastern medical treatments. The Qigong training produced a general increase in the resistance and immunological function of these patients and noticeably improved their physical condition. Thus it was empirically proven that Qigong is an approach to cancer treatment which deserves greater attention and study."

Why then is Qigong able to cure cancer? To answer this question, the explanation of Dr. Liu Gui-zhen, the foremost authority on Qigong therapy in mainland China, will be quoted.

"Naturally, it is not possible to destroy cancer cells just by practicing Qigong. Destroying cancer cells requires radiation or chemotherapy. Nevertheless, cancer patients as a rule grow quite weak in the course of treatment. Drugs and radiation therapy subsequent to surgery are especially responsible for producing side-effects such as loss of appetite, nausea, vomiting, and insomnia, as well as poor complexion and weight loss, along with a decrease in blood cells like leukocytes and platelets. As a result, patients become more and more emaciated and are unable to continue the treatments, and eventually they lose the fight against cancer. One of the main reasons patients are unable to overcome cancer is because of this decline in health and vitality in the process of cancer treatment. Qigong therapy proves very helpful in this respect by alleviating various side-effects and symptoms. Those patients who participate in Qigong therapy without exception increase their appetite and get better sleep, and further their blood count becomes normal, their complexion improves, and they gain weight. Consequently, their limbs become stronger, and they are more energetic in general, so they are more able to withstand surgery, radiation, and chemotherapy. Thus these patients stand a much better chance of overcoming cancer."

Another explanation offered by a different source states as follows:

"Qigong therapy is a wholistic approach which deals with the basic cause of the disease. While Qigong is able to cure the main ailment, what it also does is to improve the functional state of nerve control centers and correct abnormalities in various parts of the body to effect a cure in the part with the main ailment. This is the reason Qigong can cure several diseases simultaneously and can prove beneficial even in cases of cancer."

In this respect Qigong can be regarded as being similar in its effects to acupuncture since acupuncture is also thought to work by improving the functional state of nerve control centers, which in turn affect the source of the disease to bring about recovery. Since Qigong also improves circulation, stimulates metabolism, and increases resistance to disease, it is plausible that one could thus combat a terminal disease like cancer.

Rujing—The Secret to Qigong

One of the main aims in the practice of Qigong is to experience Rujing [入静] (which literally means to enter a state of quietness). Rujing is regarded as being an important step which distinguishes beginners from those who have mastered Qigong. It is difficult to describe exactly what the state of Rujing is in so many words since it is a unique experience for each person. Nevertheless, attempts have been made in Chinese literature on the subject to define it. The following are a few such descriptions:

> "A condition where the mind is completely at rest and the body is totally relaxed.
> "A process whereby the number of absent thoughts coming to mind decrease and one's attention becomes increasingly focused, although a person's thinking does not cease altogether.
> "A state attained by those practicing Qigong after they learn to dispel idle thoughts and focus their awareness. In this state one is able to remain relatively undisturbed by external stimuli such as light and sound. In some cases, people even lose their sense of body positioning or no longer feel the pull of gravity."

While Rujing mainly denotes a quiet and peaceful state, it is often associated with unusual sensations. Aside from the above descriptions, there are times when a person practicing Qigong begins to feel heavy as if he were turned into stone or as if his shoulders were being pressed down by weights. There are cases where the muscles begin to twitch or where the body begins to shake. Others have reported sensations of heat in their lower abdomen or a flow like warm liquid inside their bodies, and otherwise tingling sensations on their skin. All these things are actually an indication that the practice of Qigong is beginning to have a deep effect, so there is no need to become alarmed or try and stop such sensations since these sensations are signs that health is about to improve. Neither should one become disturbed or preoccupied with these sensations. Just remain calm and continue practicing as instructed.

What does Rujing mean in terms of the electrical activity of the brain? When a person practicing Qigong is monitored in the state of Rujing with an EEG (electro-encephalogram), alpha waves increase and theta waves also appear frequently. Alpha waves are brain waves which appear when cerebral activity is very quiet, and theta waves are characteristic of the early stages of sleep. Even though a person is wide awake, during Rujing the brain remains in a very calm state like that just preceding sleep. The study of brain wave patterns of Qigong practitioners has also shown that the cerebrum stays in a sedated state for extended periods. Maintaining the brain in a state of inhibited cerebral activity for long periods serves to restore the functioning of the brain to a normal condition after it has become overexcited or fatigued. As stated earlier, this creates conditions favorable for the regeneration of vitality throughout the whole body and for attaining one's optimum physical condition.

It usually takes some time before a beginner is able to attain Rujing, which is the first important threshold to be reached in the practice of Qigong. There are three methods which make it possible for everyone to reach this first threshold and appreciate the real benefits of Qigong. The first method is to do a little light exercise before practicing Qigong such as flexing and stretching limbs, massaging acupuncture points on the head, and rapidly opening and closing the teeth to stimulate salivation. The second way is to count the number of breaths or to focus one's awareness on breathing. For example, outgoing breaths can be counted from one to ten, and after reaching ten the same count can be repeated. Another way is to listen for the barely audible sound of the outgoing breath passing through the nose. The third method for reaching Rujing, which is to keep one's attention totally focused on one thing. One may visualize some place, person, or thing which puts one in a happy state of mind. Another approach used often is to concentrate on a specific point on the body such as Dantian, the point just below the navel, or the soles of the feet. All these methods for attaining Rujing as well as details on how to practice Qigong are covered in detail in the chapters which follow.

The Normal Effects

Special Sensations

When a person practices Qigong over a long time, some special effects or sensations are bound to be experienced from time to time. Most commonly, a special sensation is felt on the skin surface and occasionally there are mental reactions to external stimuli. There is no need for concern when such sensations arise as long as they are transient and can be easily tolerated. Some people have itching sensations in various parts of their body, while others feel as if certain parts of their body had become heavy. Otherwise, many superficial sensations such as coolness, heat, itching, or tingling occur. All these sensations are indications that one is entering Rujing or that the Qigong is having an effect. Do not become tense or worried about these sensations because they usually go away by themselves when you keep on practicing.

In the Chinese Qigong classic, Qingzuo Yaojue [静坐要訣], sixteen special sensations which result from Qigong practice are recorded. These include the superficial sensations of movement, itching, coolness, warmth, lightness, heaviness, roughness, and smoothness, as well as the feelings of falling, swaying, coldness, heat, floating, sinking, hardness, and softness. One or more of these sensations occur to differing extents in every person who practices Qigong, but usually these sensations are quite hard to define.

Another common occurrence among those who practice Qigong is unusual mental reactions. When people become very calm during Qigong and mental activity comes almost to a complete standstill, their responsiveness to external stimuli declines. As a result, sometimes people begin to hear faint noises which are not normally audible. Sometimes the sound has a physical source and other times it does not. Some people on occasion experience a floating sensation as if they were in a cloud. Others feel as if they were right on the verge of falling asleep, although they are quite awake. A person's awareness changes to where it seems as if he were being gently lifted into a different level of awareness.

It is, in fact, quite impossible to accurately describe the subjective sensations accompanying the transition into Rujing. Nevertheless it can be said that in all cases these subjective sensations are due to changes in cerebral activity. During Qigong practice the area of inhibited activity in the cerebral cortex is increased and this induces various levels of hypnosis. The wide area of inhibited cerebral activity serves as the backdrop for the special effects which occasionally occur during the practice of Qigong.

It must be emphasized that there is no need to become concerned about such effects. Furthermore, you must refrain from becoming too involved in them. All these sensations are immaterial and transitory. As long as you pay little attention to them and keep your concentration, they will eventually go away by themselves.

Improved Digestive Function

One of the most universal physical effects of continued Qigong practice is improved digestive function. Some people who practice Qigong find that their appetite increases so much that they have to eat more than the usual three meals a day. Whether this is desirable or not, all depends on the physical condition of the individual. This is a welcome development for those who are sick or weak, while this could prove to be a real nuisance for those who are overweight. Since the practice of Qigong improves digestion and absorption, this naturally causes a person to gain weight. Needless to say, those who already have weight problems should not eat between meals and should refrain from practicing Qigong in ways which incline them in this direction. Also, overweight people should increase the proportion of fruits and vegetables in their diet to keep their caloric intake at reasonable levels.

Increased Metabolic Activity

All the metabolic processes in the body become activated as a result of practicing Qigong properly. The changes brought about by increased metabolic activity varies according to the individual and the type of Qigong practiced. The most frequent response to continued practice is that the body warms up and there is some perspiration during practice. The perspiration in the palm of the hands and in the feet is usually the most noticeable. The reason people feel warmer and perspire more freely is because Qigong causes vasodilation in the extremities and increases peripheral circulation. The increased circulation which results from Qigong practice improves a person's complexion and in time facial skin becomes smoother. Also, pulse which can be felt on the wrist and just to the front of the ear become stronger and more even. Improved circulation can even cause those who have a general tendency of feeling cold to instead feel warm all over.

In most cases this warmth is not an unpleasant feeling, and a person usually feels expanded and good. The increased warmth is a normal effect of Qigong, but if the perspiration becomes excessive to wet your clothes or covers, you should wear less clothes or use less covers. Also, when perspiration is excessive, the time of Qigong practice should be reduced and the amount of concentration on Dantian point [丹田] below the navel should be decreased temporarily. Normally, your body will make the adjustment in a few days and there should be no problem with excessive perspiration.

The up-and-down movement of the tongue with breathing in Qigong causes an increase in salivation. Whenever saliva accumulates in your mouth because of this, you should swallow it. When you swallow, imagine that you are swallowing it all the way down to the lower abdomen. This will be effective in drawing your Qi downward and will aid your concentration on Dantian as well as facilitate abdominal breathing. If the amount of salivation becomes excessive and interferes with your practice, change your breathing technique to inhale through your mouth and exhale through your nose, and instead of moving your tongue up and down, just leave it in the normal position.

The increased rate of metabolic activity caused by practicing Qigong makes one's hair and nails grow faster. Also, some people experience more frequent urination. There have been cases in China where people have regained the hair on their head which they had lost in the course of their illness. Hair also often becomes darker for those with white hair who practiced Qigong regularly.

The increased metabolism also improves the distribution of nutrients throughout the body, and one's skin tends to become softer and smoother. Furthermore, scars and blemishes on the skin have a way of clearing up. There is one case in China where a patient had scrofula (tuberculosis of the lymph glands, especially those in the neck) and even after surgery there were large egg sized scars left on his neck and he was unable to raise his left arm. After forty days of intensive Qigong practice, however, the scar tissue softened and diminished considerably in size, and the patient regained freedom of movement in his right arm.

All of the above mentioned physical changes including the feeling of warmth all over, increased perspiration, more frequent urination, faster growth of hair and nails, as well as softer and clearer skin, are normal effects resulting from heightened metabolic function, and there is no need to become concerned over such physical changes. Just continue practicing regularly, and these effects will stabilize and you will become accustomed to these usually welcome changes.

Greater Sexual Response

After practicing Qigong over a long period, people usually improve their physical condition substantially, and their alertness and level of physical energy progressively increase. Along with this some people experience an increase in sexual drive.
This is a natural physiological phenomena, but some moderation is in order. Sexual intercourse greatly excites the central nervous system and affects the balance between mental and physical functions. Thus sex can be initially disadvantageous for Qigong training because it can go against the aim of establishing harmony between one's mind and body. Having sex while still recovering from illness has a way of depleting physical energy, which could otherwise be used for restoring normal physiological functions, and can thus prolong the recovery period.

Concerning nocturnal emission in men, once or twice a month (for a young man, once a week) is normal, and there is no need to be concerned about this. Those who have nocturnal emission too frequently or those who have just had emission should use the method detailed below to consolidate their energy before practicing Qigong.

First, close the eyes and focus attention on the very top of the head and inhale after touching the tip of the tongue on the hard palate. Contract the anal sphincter muscles to pull the anus in and draw up the testicles. Hold the breath as long as possible after inhaling and then exhale and start all over again. Incidences of nocturnal emission will decrease and eventually cease when this exercise is done on a regular basis.

Also, when one is about to have emission, one can prevent this by firmly pressing the perineum (just between the anus and the back of the testicles) with the middle finger. Those who have nocturnal emission too frequently should make a regular practice of constricting their anal sphincter muscles (as if trying to prevent a bowel movement) for at least one minute everyday. Also it is beneficial to perform the Dantian Rub exercise (see page 86) while holding the testicles, once a day in the morning and once at night. One may also press the perineum up to ten times after this exercise. Regular practice of these methods along with Qigong will effectively reduce nocturnal emission.

Effects of Qigong on Women

In some cases practicing Qigong influences the menstrual cycle. Qigong may be practiced as usual during menstrual periods as long as there is no change in the menstrual period or in the quantity of menstrual flow. If the period lengthens or the quantity of flow increases, women must change their point of concentration from Dantian below the navel to Shanzhong [膻中] (midpoint of the nipples) or the sole of their feet. Otherwise, women should give up concentrating on one point during their period. Women should not make their Qi reach Dantian during their menstrual period because this tends to increase menstrual flow. Holding the breath in any way also has an undesirable effect for menstruating women. When the menstrual period lengthens or the flow is excessive, despite changing the method, women should discontinue Qigong practice for several days until their period is over.

There is a general tendency for the menstrual period to come early for the first few months after taking up Qigong, but there is no cause for concern. The amount of menstrual flow also changes for some women after three or four months of regular Qigong practice. This is a result of natural adjustments of the body, and there is nothing to worry about. Women who are past their menopause can concentrate on Dantian as much as they wish.

Women who are pregnant or breast-feeding can practice Vitalizing Qigong (see page 62) without any ill effects, but they must not practice Inner Regulation Qigong (see page 50) after the third month of pregnancy. If a woman is pregnant and has head-aches or a dull sensation in her head when practicing Qigong, she must switch her point of concentration from Dantian to Shanzhong.

Compared with men, women tend to breathe more with their chest, and sometimes abdominal breathing is difficult, especially for pregnant women. If this is the case, Qigong can be practiced with the normal way of breathing. Women should not force themselves to breathe abdominally. Instead they should allow themselves an ample amount of time to gradually change over to abdominal breathing. Everyone can learn to breathe abdominally; it is only a matter of time. There is no reason to hurry.

Falling Asleep

Some people become very drowsy when practicing Qigong, especially in the lying postures, and sometimes people fall fast asleep. This is caused by lying down and closing the eyes in a quiet and relaxing atmosphere. Obviously this is very conducive to sleep, and it is quite natural that a person should fall asleep under these conditions. When a person falls asleep, however, the benefits of Qigong are lost. Also drowsiness is a hindrance to reaching the special state of inhibited cerebral activity called Rujing where the mind is at still but completely alert.

To keep from falling asleep, instead of closing your eyes all the way, keep them slightly open just enough to admit one thin streak of light. If you become drowsy during practice, change your posture as often as necessary to stay awake. It is also helpful to drink some tea before starting to practice Qigong.

Involuntary Movements

Many people experience involuntary movements during the practice of Qigong, particularly after practicing for a few months. Spontaneous movements occur inde-pendent of a person's intentions and occur especially in the limbs after a person learns to relax completely. The movements vary greatly from person to person: Sometimes they are small shaking movements and sometimes they are large thrashing movements. In Qigong, this is called the "involuntary movement response." So far, no clear explanation has been offered as to why such movements occur. It is worth noting, however, that many patients undergoing Qigong therapy in Chinese hospitals report a sense of relief after allowing such involuntary movements to take their course. So generally this type of movement is seen as a sign of progress, and it is regarded as being an automatic adjusting mechanism of the body.

Therefore, if involuntary movements begin, you should allow it to take place, neither trying to encourage it nor stop it. However, if the movement becomes excessive or out of hand, or if it causes discomfort and aggravates physical symptoms, you should stop the movement. Normally, changing the point of concentration to the lower Dantian (the perineum) or Yongquan (point on the middle of the soles) is enough to stop involuntary movement. Also, changing your posture from standing to sitting or lying, or vice versa, usually brings involuntary movement to a stop. Do not worry even if some movements should still persist, as long as it does not disturb your concentration. When large involuntary movements occur every time Qigong is practiced, one should stop practicing Qigong for a certain period. There is no need to be concerned about such involuntary movement. Just think of it as your body going through a process of adjustment.

The Abnormal Effects

There are times when a person experiences abnormal or undesirable effects during the practice of Qigong. The type of reaction that appears varies according to the individual, but such abnormal effects never occur at all for most people. Nevertheless, since these abnormal reactions do occur on occasion, the more common ones will be listed and explained so that you will be able to avoid them and know what to do in case they should happen to you.

Exhaustion

When one's posture is unnatural or one remains in the same position for a long time, sometimes certain muscles become strained and fatigued, and this can cause some people to feel exhausted and weak all over. For this reason, one should pay close attention to make sure that the posture is comfortable and the body can be kept completely relaxed. Fatigue is one reason beginners to Qigong are advised against practicing for a long time. Until one learns how to relax completely, keeping the same posture for extended periods can be quite tiresome. Therefore, beginners should take breaks during long practice sessions and adjust their posture so that they are comfortable.

Those who are seriously ill or are in a weakened and emaciated condition should practice in the lying postures until they have regained their strength. The sitting and standing postures should be used only after recovering completely. This will reduce fatigue and prevent exhaustion.

Shortness of Breath

Some people become short of breath during Qigong practice, experience discomfort in their chest, or feel an obstruction in the pit of their stomach. This causes their breathing to become labored and strained. Such breathing difficulties are generally caused by attempting to maintain the same position despite discomfort, by pushing the chest too far forward, by bending forward at the waist, by breathing unnaturally, by holding the breath for too long, or by trying to breathe too deeply. If you find that you are becoming short of breath, relax and just breathe in whatever way comes naturally. Then you can correct the cause of the problem. Do not rush yourself, but instead allow yourself an ample amount of time to master the breathing techniques.

Palpitations

Some people experience palpitation during Qigong practice. Generally this is caused by not being able to relax in a given posture, by forcing the breathing, or by making the pauses between each breath too long. Often people who experience palpitations are too tense to begin with. Otherwise, it happens that too many words are used for the special phrase, and this makes breathing difficult. One must correct these causes in order to alleviate this condition.

People who have functional and structural heart disorders tend to have a rapid pulse, and often they have palpitations even under normal circumstances. Naturally for these people palpitations are more likely to occur during Qigong practice. These people should take special care to practice Qigong in a comfortable position and to continue practice only as long as they can do so in a relaxed manner. The more a person learns to relax, the less tendency there will be for palpitations.

Pain and Discomfort in the Abdomen

Sometimes pain and discomfort in the abdominal area is experienced by beginners to Qigong. This is usually caused by forcing one's breathing to be too deep or by making the abdominal wall expand and contract unnaturally. Also, when people have gastrointestinal problems, practicing Qigong can cause symptoms such as abdominal pain, a feeling of distention in the abdomen, or diarrhea. If this is the case, one must first receive proper medical attention before beginning to practice Qigong and should always keep in mind one's physical limitations when practicing. Even if the practice time is kept relatively short to avoid discomfort in the abdomen, regular Qigong practice will strengthen the digestive system and such symptoms should cease to occur after a while.

Being Startled or Frightened

Sometimes people practicing Qigong become startled or frightened by hearing sudden and unexpected loud sounds nearby, by something jolting them without warning, or by having some hallucination. When this happens, people often become jittery and remain nervous and tense long after the initial cause has disappeared. Some people even become dazed and enervated.

One good way to prevent such surprises while you are practicing Qigong in a state of deep relaxation and concentration is to make sure to practice in a place where you can remain undisturbed and loud noises are unlikely to disrupt your practice.

Even if some disruption should occur, it is important to minimize its effect as much as you can by keeping your composure and holding your concentration on Dantian. As long as the disturbance is minor, it is better to relax totally, continue practicing, and reestablish your concentration. Nevertheless, if some hallucination occurs which is too difficult to bear, quickly bring the practice to a close and resume practice some other time.

Dizziness and Headaches

There are people who begin to feel heat in their lower abdomen or low back area after practicing Qigong for a certain period. Sometimes people feel this heat traveling up the spine to reach the top of their head. Under ideal circumstances, the sensation of heat subsequently travels down the front centerline of the body to return to the lower abdomen. This is the circulation of energy along the Governor and Conception Vessels as will be explained later; the practice of intentionally circulating energy this way is known as Zhoutian Gong [周天功]. This phenomena, when it occurs spontaneously without any complications, is good for a one's health and is very beneficial in terms of curing diseases and restoring vitality.

Nevertheless, when people consciously try to cause this circulation of energy in the belief that they have to achieve this circulation in order to benefit from Qigong, various problems are likely to occur. Trying to induce this circulation actually does more harm than good, and sometimes forcing energy up the spine causes energy to become blocked in the head. This can cause sensations of dizziness as well as a feeling of oppression and pain in the head. The preponderance of energy in the upper regions of the body can also cause anxiety and irritability.

If such symptoms should occur, you should not try to move the energy and must keep the tongue on the hard palate and concentrate either on the soles of the feet or the big toes. If these symptoms persist, you must discontinue Qigong practice altogether for a number of days and you should only resume practice after these symptoms disappear completely.

Relapse of Illness

Almost everyone experiences definite improvement in various physical symptoms and feel stronger and more energetic after practicing Qigong regularly for several months. It does happen for some people, however, that their illnesses or symptoms become temporarily worse in the course of Qigong practice. It is usual for there to be a period of instability in the process of recovering from an illness. Nevertheless, it is only reasonable that medical care should be sought to determine the cause and prevent the illness from getting even worse when there is a relapse or a marked deterioration in a person's condition.

For example, even if a person who had an ulcer finds complete relief from his symptoms after practicing Qigong for several months, if he overworks, experiences a great amount of stress, or eats too many of the wrong kinds of food, the pain is likely to return. In cases like this, it is important to find the cause of the relapse and to work on eliminating this so that the therapeutic effects of Qigong are not undermined. In rare cases, a patient with an ulcer will experience a sudden relapse while practicing Qigong, such as perforation and internal bleeding. This calls for emergency medical care without delay. Qigong, however, is rarely the direct cause of a relapse, so once the individual has sufficiently recovered, Qigong is recommended along with conventional medical treatments. In the great majority of cases, this will speed the recovery and facilitate rehabilitation.

It must be emphasized, however, that when a person fails to deal with the original causes of the relapse, such as, irregular living habits, exposure to the elements, overworking, immoderation in eating and drinking, and poor mental health, this sows the seeds for another relapse. Discontinuing the practice of Qigong also increases the chances of a relapse. Continuing to practice Qigong regularly assures a person of the best chances for complete recovery.

The most desirable thing is for a person to keep practicing Qigong even after completely recovering from an illness, which is exactly what most patients who undergo Qigong therapy in China do. The majority of patients who recover with the help of Qigong incorporate Qigong practice into their daily routine. The salutary effects of Qigong are a well-established fact. Taking an active interest in the maintenance of health and the prevention of disease in this way greatly enhances and consolidates the body's ability to remain healthy. Not only can one prevent the recurrence of illness by practicing Qigong, but one can enjoy an abundance of physical and mental energy and live a more productive and fulfilling life.

Qigong and Diet

For those who are undertaking Qigong practice for the purpose of recovering from their physical problems, modifying their diet to improve digestion and absorption becomes an important factor. The benefits of practicing Qigong can be multiplied by modifying one's diet and eating habits to complement the effects of Qigong. Practicing Qigong increases the range of movement in the diaphragm, and this has a massaging effect on the organs in the abdominal cavity. The metabolic processes of the internal organs are thus activated and in turn increase the peristaltic movements of the stomach and intestines.

In cases where a person is underweight and in poor physical condition, it is important that one get something to eat when becoming hungry after practicing Qigong.

This will assure good digestion and assimilation. This healthy appetite will eventually be lost if food is not eaten when one is hungry. Losing this chance for good digestion will adversely affect the recovery of one's physical condition and consequently prolong the cure of the disease.

While the actual diet eaten may be varied according to individual needs and preferences, it is desirable that one eat foods high in protein such as meat, eggs, and dairy products, when conditions permit. This will aid the strengthening of one's physical condition. Even those with serious gastrointestinal disorders may eat once between breakfast and lunch and once between lunch and supper. As long as one has an appetite and meals are kept reasonably small, this will not be a burden on the digestive system.

On the other hand, those who have weight problems, hypertension, or cardiovascular disorders must pay attention to keeping their weight down so as not to adversely affect their chances of recovery. For this purpose, people with weight problems should limit their diet and switch to a low fat and low carbohydrate diet and eat more fruits and vegetables.

There are two main rules regarding eating and Qigong: The first rule is not to practice Inner Regulation Qigong (page 50) on an empty stomach and the second is not to practice Vitalizing Qigong (page 62) on a full stomach. Inner Regulation Qigong markedly improves the function of the digestive organs. Thus, when Inner Regulation Qigong is practiced on an empty stomach, the feeling of hunger tends to become even greater. Hunger can become a big obstacle to entering the state of Rujing. Although Inner Regulation Qigong has the effect of improving digestion and absorption, this effect does not benefit a person when practiced on an empty stomach. The proper timing for meals and the practice of Inner Regulation Qigong is very important for those with gastrointestinal problems.

There is also good reason for not practicing Vitalizing Qigong on a full stomach. The upper abdomen is full just after a meal, and because Vitalizing Qigong is usally practiced seated in the cross-legged position, this makes it difficult to concentrate on Dantian, which is located in the lower abdomen. For this reason, allow at least an hour after a meal before beginning to practice Vitalizing Qigong.

Another point of caution for people with weakened digestive systems such as those with gastroptosis is not to practice Stepping Qigong or any other type of Qigong exercise in the standing position right after a meal. Practicing Qigong in the standing position with a full stomach will increase the downward displacement of the stomach. This impedes the normal passage of food from the stomach to the intestines and aggravates the condition of gastroptosis.

Qigong for the Seriously Ill

Those who are seriously ill should take leave of their responsibilities so that they can devote themselves to the practice of Qigong. If possible, these people should get a complete break from having to attend to all the little details that need to be taken care of in life. In China seriously ill people in hospitals are able to receive special training from Qigong experts and are thus able to speed up their recovery and shorten their period of convalescence under the guidance of physicians. Such ideal cooperation with medical professionals is not usually possible in Western countries. Nevertheless, even without the help of Qigong experts, one can practice on one's own to obtain similar results. The most important factor for success with Qigong in any situation is diligent practice by the individual. One only needs to find a quiet room to practice in and to practice at a time of day when one is relatively relaxed and at ease.

People who are seriously ill and those who have problems related to the reproductive organs, such as spermatorrhea in men or endometritis in women, should strictly abstain from sex. Sexual activity greatly excites the central nervous system and a substantial amount of physical energy needed to restore proper physiological functions is expended. Therefore, sex can have a negative influence on the recovery of health. Ancient Qigong masters are known to have forbidden their students from having sex for the first one hundred days after beginning training. The purpose behind this was to conserve vital energy and make surplus energy available to activate powerful internal mechanisms. Abstinence was demanded for good reason—to assure that one's inner resources would be developed quickly and surely.

Indications and Contra-indications

The scope of diseases treatable with Qigong therapy encompasses a very wide range as may be expected from the foregoing explanations on the general effects of Qigong. Since Qigong has the beneficial effects as mentioned, aside from being an asset in improving one's constitution, building health, and preventing diseases, Qigong therapy can be regarded as being effective for almost all chronic diseases. Among these, however, there are a number of diseases for which Qigong has been found to be particularly effective. In the first eight years of Dr. Liu's experience with Qigong therapy, he listed just fifteen diseases as being specially indicated for Qigong. By 1966, however, this list of "indicated" diseases grew to as many as eighty. In the revised Chinese edition of *Practical Qigong Therapy* by Dr. Liu Gui-zhen (1981), the kinds of Qigong to be practiced as well as other special recommendations are detailed for sixty-seven of these diseases. An abridged version of these recommendations are presented in Chapter 5 of this book.

Therefore, what follows is just a partial list of the diseases for which Qigong has been found to be effective. Even among the diseases below for which Qigong therapy is specially effective, there are those for which Qigong is more effective than others. Therefore, the diseases are listed roughly in order of effectiveness under each heading.

Digestive Disorders—duodenal and gastric ulcers, gastroptosis, chronic hepatitis, liver cirrhosis
Respiratory Disorders—bronchial asthma, pulmonary tuberculosis
Circulatory Disorders—hypertension, heart diseases such as coronary arteriosclerosis
Nervous Disorders—neurasthenia, autonomic ataxia
Reproductive Disorders—dysmenorrhea, impotence

As for chronic hepatitis and liver cirrhosis, it takes time before improvement is seen, but the effects of Qigong therapy are cumulative over time, and it has been clinically verified that the progression of these diseases can be halted or at the very least be slowed down. The effect of Qigong for other serious diseases such as tuberculosis, hypertension, and diabetes is also comparatively gradual but consistent.

Perhaps the most remarkable thing about Qigong therapy, as discussed earlier, is that it is able to bring about remissions in various malignancies. Qigong has thus been proven effective for a wide variety of diseases ranging from relatively mild ones to serious and even terminal cases.

There are, however, conditions for which Qigong is not recommended (contra-indications), and these should be carefully noted before attempting the practice of Qigong. The contra-indications are as follows:

(1) All diseases in the acute stage
(2) Recovery period after major surgery
(3) Retinal bleeding
(4) Severe bronchitis
(5) Severe hematemesis (vomiting of blood)
(6) Respiratory problems associated with serious diseases
(7) Postpartum period (just after childbirth)
(8) Mental illnesses

Chapter 2

General Guidelines of Qigong

The Basic Principles

The Fine Points of Diaoshen (Adjust Posture)

The posture assumed in the practice of Qigong is one of the basic elements in this Chinese exercise system. It is important that everyone select the right postures for Qigong practice according to one's physical condition or personal habits and preferences. The position of the body has a definite influence on the function of the internal organs. To illustrate how one's body position can influence the function of internal organs, the effect of different postures on the function of the stomach will be briefly examined below.

Standing posture: Those with normal stomach function show a fairly even distribution of food material along the entire digestive tract while standing. This means that the peristaltic action of the intestines and stomach is smooth and rhythmical and that one's bowel movements are regular. For those with stomach problems such as ulcers and gastroptosis, however, peristaltic action of the stomach is weak and slow. When this is the case, food material tends to collect in the lower end of the stomach and in the duodenum. When the density of the food is great, food material even backtracks into the stomach. It stands to reason, therefore, that those who have stomach problems should not practice Qigong in the standing posture.

Sitting posture: The shape and the action of the stomach is generally much the same in the sitting postures as it is in standing postures. The movement of stomach contents in the sitting posture, therefore, display the same tendency as that in the standing posture. For some individuals, however, the cross-legged seated position increases the internal pressure within the abdominal cavity to some extent and this in turn increases the tonicity of the stomach.

Lying posture: The peristaltic action of the stomach and intestines generally increases when a person lays down to rest. This principle can be applied to the benefit of those with digestive problems in the practice of Qigong. When a person assumes the side-lying posture with the right side down, this places the stomach, which is on the left side of the abdominal cavity, above the pylorus and duodenum. Gravity acts to draw food out through the pylorus into the duodenum in this position to facilitate the movement of food material through the digestive tract. This is beneficial for those with gastrointestinal problems whose peristaltic action is weak and slow. People with digestive problems can therefore get the best results by practicing Qigong in the side-lying position with their right side down.

From the above discussion, it can be understood how posture really does affect physiological functions. The choice of body position for practicing Qigong basically depends upon how one wishes to affect the function of the internal organs. The benefits of certain postures for particular types of diseases, however, are relative, and one must arrive at the best posture through practical experience. Some general guidelines for selecting the right body position for Qigong practice will be given below so that you can choose the best posture for yourself.

Those who are old and weak, those who are seriously ill and debilitated, those who have a weak stomach so that it takes a long time to pass food and liquids through their system, and those who have ulcers, gastroptosis, tuberculosis, or heart disease should practice Qigong primarily in one of the lying postures. Practicing in a lying posture conserves energy and prevents fatigue. Also, since practicing in a lying posture increases peristaltic action, this can improve the appetite for those with a poor appetite.

·Those who are in relatively good physical condition, those who are only slightly ill, those who are almost recovered from an illness, those who have an overactive stomach and feel discomfort in their chest and sides along with a heavy sensation in their head, and those with high blood pressure, neurasthenia, or a tendency to fall asleep in the sitting and lying postures should practice Qigong primarily in a standing posture. Any one of the sitting postures can be used by the majority of people except those who are in an extremely emaciated condition.

Qigong can be performed in all types of postures including lying, sitting, and standing postures. The essential point in assuming any position is that you are able to maintain it for a extended period in a relaxed and natural manner. Sometimes maintaining one posture for a long time is difficult for a person. The following advice is therefore offered for each type of posture so that you will be able to stay comfortable in your chosen position.

Lying posture: The lying posture includes the supine, side-lying, and reclining positions. The head has to be raised slightly with a pillow in the case of the supine position because this increases comfort and facilitates breathing. In the side-lying position, as stated before, digestion is improved when you lie with the right side down. As long as you are not practicing on a full stomach, however, it does not matter whether you lie on the right or left side. It is possible to alternate between lying on the right side and the left side. In both the supine and side-lying positions it is best to lay on a hard surface instead of on a soft bed. Lying on a bed or sofa in these positions makes it difficult to maintain the correct posture.

In the case of the reclining position, however, reclining on a soft bed or sofa poses no problem. Lying on a soft seat or couch is actually a very good way to assume the reclining position. Just stretch out on the chair or couch and lean your head on the backrest and relax. Keep your arms and legs stretched out and completely relaxed. When assuming the reclining position on a bed or the floor, one must place some blankets and pillows under one's head and shoulders to raise them up. The legs should be kept naturally straight and the arms should be placed out to the side totally relaxed. The reclining position is most suited to those with heart problems or bronchitis. Respiration is easier in this position and it prevents labored breathing and discomfort in the chest area. This posture is ideal for anyone in a weak condition or in times when you have become tired after practicing a long time in the standing or seated postures.

The supine and side-lying positions are most suited to beginners of Qigong and those who are physically weak. After two or three weeks of practice, when you have mastered the basic breathing technique, you can start practicing Qigong in the seated postures. The lying and seated postures can be used alternately thereafter according to your own preference and convenience. If you cannot get used to practicing in any of the seated postures, it is possible to practice exclusively in one of the lying postures.

Seated posture: The seated posture includes sitting in a cross-legged position on the floor as well as sitting on a chair or stool. Vitalizing Qigong is usually practiced in one of the cross-legged positions. The seated postures are quite simple, but they are only suited to those who are in relatively good physical condition. Those who have recovered their health after an illness may also practice in the cross-legged positions.

It often happens that those who practice Qigong in the cross-legged position for the first time experience some discomfort or pain in their legs. If this is the case, you can cross the legs the other way or interrupt the Qigong practice temporarily to walk around a bit and restore circulation in the legs. When the legs become very numb, you may also massage them. Beginners should place a cushion or some padding underneath their hips when assuming the cross-legged position in order to keep the legs from going to sleep. The amount of time you are able to remain in the cross-legged position will increase with practice, and eventually sitting cross-legged on the floor for a long time will pose no problem.

When practicing Qigong by sitting on a chair or stool, it is important that the chair be just the right height so that your knees are bent at a right angle and your thighs are parallel with the floor. You can place something on the chair to raise the sitting height, or otherwise place something under your feet to adjust your posture. Also, it is important that your spine be kept straight. It is difficult for beginners to relax while keeping their back straight. Remember, therefore, to push your hips back and thrust your lower abdomen forward and keep your attention focused on Dantain. It is always easier to keep the upper half of the body relaxed and upright if your energy is concentrated at Dantian.

Standing posture: Only one basic standing position, with the feet about shoulder-width apart and the knees slightly bent, has been introduced in this book. There are, however, several variations in the positioning of the arms. The standing position is primarily for those who are physically fit and unlikely to tire easily. Nevertheless, practicing for more than thirty minutes in the standing position can cause fatigue in beginners. If you become unable to relax in the standing position, it is better to bring the exercise to an end and assume a posture in which you are able to relax completely to continue with a breathing exercise of your choice.

The main thing to remember about the standing position is to keep the upper body relaxed and to concentrate on Dantian or your feet. Your shoulders and arms should be kept relaxed and loose. Even when holding the arms out in front of Dantian or your chest, it should be done with the minimum possible effort. If the effort causes fatigue in your arms and shoulders, drop your arms down to your side and let your shoulders down. The key to maintaining the standing position effortlessly is your stance and concentration on Dantian; the position of the arms is always secondary.

No matter which posture you practice in, the main criterion for your choice of positions should be that you are able to remain completely relaxed in that position. You have to be able to relax all your muscles, and breathe in a relaxed and natural manner; you must not become fatigued. If you feel discomfort in any part of your body during Qigong practice, you should correct your posture or otherwise bring the practice to a close and start over again at a later time.

One single position is not always indicated for a particular disease. Often several body positions are used alternately for the best results. When a person has several diseases, it is possible to alternate between several postures. For example, if a person has both gastroptosis and hypertension, he could use the side-lying position on the right side when practicing shortly after a meal, and he could use a sitting posture between meals. The kind of postures used should be selected to suit individual conditions and should be modified according to the results. When a particular position is used for a certain period and it is found that this causes fatigue or is not desirable for some reason, switch to another position without hesitation.

If you practice in a cross-legged position, for example, and find that your legs always become numb, change to sitting on a stool or chair. Otherwise, if lying on one side causes discomfort, try lying on the other side; if neither side is good, assume the reclining position. It is important that you do not put up with discomfort, but instead modify your posture as soon as you realize that it is not right for you. It is also useful to try out a certain posture for a few minutes before beginning practice to make sure that it feels right to you.

Some people easily become drowsy and fall asleep when practicing Qigong in the lying postures. If this is the case, these people should switch from the lying posture to the sitting or standing postures halfway through their Qigong practice. Conversely, if people have difficulty in quieting the mind in the standing or sitting postures, they can switch midway through practice to a lying posture. It is important to be flexible and ready to change your posture during the course of practice. Also, it is acceptable to use a different posture in each practice session during the day. The main point is to assume a position in which you are able to relax completely and quiet your mind. Diaoshen, or adjusting the posture, is just a matter of finding the right posture to suit your own condition and circumstances.

Your preference for certain postures is naturally related to your physical condition, life-style, and habits. Some people prefer to practice lying down, while others prefer to practice in the seated or standing postures. It is best to follow your own preferences so long as there are no special problems which prevent this such as injuries or disease. Most often, the posture which feels the best to you is the best posture in which to practice Qigong.

The Fine Points of Diaoxi (Regulate Breath)

Diaoxi, or regulation of breathing, is one of the basic principles underlying Qigong. When the principle of Diaoxi is practiced correctly, this will greatly increase the therapeutic effect of Qigong. If practiced incorrectly, however, the effects could be diminished. It is therefore very important that you pay careful attention when first learning the breathing techniques to practice them correctly. Therefore, some of the fine points of Diaoxi will be explained here.

The very first rule to remember in Diaoxi is that breathing must remain natural and unstrained. Instead of inhaling quickly or forcefully, you should inhale just the usual amount slowly and evenly. Your breathing can become strained if more than the usual amount of air is inhaled in an effort to breathe deeply. This makes it more difficult to place a short pause between each inhalation and exhalation. Also, the exhalation, instead of being quick or forceful, should be steady and natural. If the exhalation is made purposely strong when breathing through the nose, the excessive stimulation of air rushing through the nasal cavity can cause unnecessary discomfort. Exhaling forcefully also makes it more difficult to pause briefly before drawing another breath. A short pause should come naturally and effortlessly after each inhalation and exhalation. You should never force or strain yourself to stop breathing just to put a pause after an inhalation or exhalation. Only place a short pause when it is easy. During the momentary pause between each breath, direct your attention to your lower abdomen. It is important that you do not hold your breath in your throat or chest because side-effects such as dizziness, feeling of constriction in the chest area, or stomach pains could result.

The rate of breathing during Qigong practice is entirely up to each individual. Trying to breathe at a set rate generally produces more problems and discomfort than benefits. The average respiration rate for normal adult males is about fifteen times a minute; for women the average is about eighteen times a minute. People who regularly engage in vigorous cardiovascular exercise generally have greater lung capacity and a slower respiration rate. People who have practiced Qigong for a long time also tend to breathe at a slower rate. Even beginners in Qigong experience some slowing of respiration rate while they are practicing. It is not unusual for the respiration rate to become as low as four or five per minute while practicing Qigong after regular practice. The respiration rate during practice even gets as low as one or two per minute for some people. It is impossible, however, for a beginner to breathe so slowly and deeply without a special effort. You must always remain true to your own natural breathing capacity and practice with the aim of making gradual and steady progress. Remember that there is no direct corelation between a slow respiration rate and the benefits of Qigong. Therefore, there is no need to try and reduce your respiration rate intentionally. Just breathe in a relaxed and comfortable way and try to keep your breath calm, steady, and silent.

People usually breathe through their nose during Qigong practice, but it is also possible to breathe through both the nose and the mouth. Those who have nasal problems may initially choose to breathe exclusively through their mouth. Those with respiratory problems can begin practicing Qigong by breathing in whatever way is the most comfortable for them. Whether to breathe through the nose, the mouth, or both the nose and the mouth in Qigong practice depends on the breathing technique employed. In Relaxation Qigong, breathing through the nose only is recommended, but this is not a requirement. In Vitalizing Qigong also, you breathe through the nose only, but again, this is not mandatory. In Inner Regulation Qigong and Stepping Qigong, generally you inhale through the nose and exhale through the mouth. Breathing only through the mouth is not usually done in Qigong, but this option is open to those who cannot breathe comfortably otherwise.

One of the most important objectives in Diaoxi is mastering abdominal, or diaphragmatic, breathing. Nevertheless, it takes years of practice to learn to breathe diaphragmatically without any effort. Therefore, it is important not to become impatient about reaching this goal. Abdominal breathing is achieved in Qigong by visualizing your breath being drawn down into the lower abdomen. The movement of the lower abdomen accompanying respiration is not very noticeable in beginners. Only after repeatedly practicing the breathing techniques while visualizing your breath being drawn down to the abdomen will the lower abdomen begin to move naturally with your breathing.

The time it takes to achieve natural abdominal breathing varies according to the individual, but generally it takes at least a month of regular practice. There are those who have prior experience with other breathing or meditation techniques. These people are usually able to begin breathing abdominally without effort much sooner. People like this are in a much better position to benefit immediately from the practice of Qigong.

In all cases, however, one must concentrate on the movement of the lower abdomen accompanying breathing. In abdominal breathing, the diaphragm is pushed down with each inhalation and this causes the abdomen to expand. Conversely, the diaphragm is raised up with each exhalation and this causes the abdomen to contract. Although the entire abdomen tends to move in unison as you breathe diaphragmatically, you must place special emphasis on the movement of the lower abdominal area. Everyone, without exception, has to start by laying stress on breathing into the lower abdomen during Qigong practice.

Moving the abdominal muscles in and out intentionally in a mechanical fashion will not do. Even if you finds a way of keeping the upper abdomen from moving and are able to move just the muscles of the lower abdomen, this will not really be beneficial unless it is a natural result of relaxed breathing. The most important objective in Diaoxi is the profound salutary effects brought about by the gradual changes in your breathing pattern. The method, or the intentional pattern dictated by the breathing technique, is of less importance than the goal of reaching a state where abdominal breathing becomes natural and effortless. Everyone will reach this state after a certain period of practice, so there is no need to become anxious.

In addition to practicing abdominal breathing, people who have problems with hypertension, constipation, indigestion, ulcers, or gastroptosis should try to make each exhalation just a little longer. They do not need to concern themselves about the amount of inhalation. They should place emphasis on the exhalation and to allow the inhalation to occur naturally.

Conversely, those who have problems with hypotension, diarrhea, enteritis, or nervous disorders should make a special attempt to inhale more fully. They do not need to concern themselves with the length of exhalation. They should place emphasis on the inhalation and to allow the exhalation to occur naturally.

Another rule of Diaoxi for people with hypertension is not to place a pause between their inhalation and exhalation. This is because some people have a tendency of holding their breath during these pauses, and this could cause an increase in vascular tension and raise the blood pressure even more.

After continued practice at visualizing your breath being drawn down into your lower abdomen, you will begin to feel a definite sensation of your breath reaching and filling your lower abdomen. This is what is known in Qigong as "Qi penetrating Dantian." The sensation of energy filling your lower abdomen will be tentative and fleeting in the beginning. If you continue to practice regularly, however, this sensation will become more distinct and enduring. Therefore, there is no need to rush this process or to intentionally tense your lower abdomen in an attempt to create this condition. You should proceed carefully remembering never to force yourself since this can cause undesirable side-effects and because forcing things goes against the spirit of Qigong.

The Fine Points of Diaoxin (Calm Mind)

The important psychological principle in Qigong is to clear one's mind of all ir-relevant thoughts and achieve the state of Rujing. Rujing refers to a condition where the mind has become very quiet and all attention is focused on one thing. This does not necessarily mean that all mental activity comes to a complete stop. There is a clear relationship between how much the mind is quieted down and how well the Qigong practice goes. Conversely, the more successful one is with Qigong practice and the longer one practices, the easier it becomes to achieve Rujing. By the same token, the sooner a person is able to enter into this state, the greater the therapeutic effects.

The main obstacle in the way of beginners trying to achieve Rujing is distracting thoughts coming up at random. One of the best ways to keep your mind from getting sidetracked during Qigong practice is to stop doing everything that engages your mind, such as watching television or reading a book, ten minutes before you begin Qigong practice. Going immediately from some other activity to Qigong practice keeps your conscious mind in an excited state and keeps you from achieving a calm and quiet mental state vital for the successful practice of Qigong. Always allow a short time period before Qigong practice to set aside those things which normally keep you occupied in life.

Also, as much as possible, place yourself in a happy and carefree mood. You can do this by listening to some pleasant music, visualizing some pleasant scenery or event, or by any other method which works to put you in a good frame of mind.

Being in a cheerful mood will facilitate a smooth transition to deeper respiration and a serene state of mind.

Many methods have been employed by monks and ascetics through history for dispelling absent thoughts, which inevitably arise in the act of contemplation. Staring at the tip of one's nose is one such method. In this method, rather than using the eyes to stare at the tip of the nose, one should just keep his attention fixed on the tip of his nose. One must avoid crossing his eyes to gaze fixedly at his nose. Overworking the eyes in this way could produce eyestrain, which in turn could cause a headache or a sensation of heaviness over the head. Needless to say, this would be counterproductive to the aim of entering the state of Rujing.

It takes very little effort to keep your gaze on your nose, as long as you keep your eyes half closed while looking at the tip of your nose. Even when you decide to use some other method of concentration, it is a good idea to keep your eyes half closed or just barely open. This is because it is hard for beginners to enter Rujing with their eyes wide open, and conversely, when the eyes are closed completely, the tendency is to fall asleep or to become lost in thought. The main point is to keep your attention focused on one point and not to let your mind wander so that you may readily attain Rujing.

Yishou Dantian [意守丹田], as explained in detail later, is the most reliable and widely practiced method for warding off distracting thoughts and achieving a calm and quiet state. Simply keep focusing your attention on Dantian below your navel, and do not allow yourself to become caught up in any absent thoughts which come up in your mind. This may be difficult at first, and absent thoughts may continue to sidetrack you. Even if this is the case, do not become too concerned about it. This happens to most beginners, so just keep on practicing. Whenever you realize your mind has been wandering, just guide it back to Dantian, or whatever you had been concentrating on, and feel the ebb and flow of your breath through this point of concentration.

Dantian, which is just below the navel, is the preferred point of concentration because it is a relatively easy place to keep one's attention focused, and in the process of concentrating on Dantian, Qi is drawn downward to induce the state of Rujing. If you find it difficult to keep your attention focused on this point, you may choose any other point on your body which serves to relax and calm your mind. This point can be inside your body or on the surface, but it is most desirable if it can be felt to move with each breath. Usually this is a point somewhere in the abdomen or chest area.

It is possible, also, to concentrate on some external object such as the moon, a star, a tree, or some plant. The main point is to keep your attention fixed on one thing to reduce mental activity to a bare minimum and reach a calm and quiet state.

Even though you are "concentrating" on a point like Dantian, this does not mean that you should become all tense about it. The trick is to avoid undue effort and to hold your attention on this point as lightly and gently as you can.

If it so happens that you are just not able to keep your concentration for some reason, bring the Qigong practice to an end and try again some other time. After you learn to concentrate on Dantian, such incidents will become less frequent, and a passing thought or two will no longer distract you the way they used to. This will in turn lead to greater powers of concentration and you will become able to attain the calm and quiet state of Rujing with ease.

Repeating a special phrase, as discussed later, is an excellent device for quieting your mind. The repetition of a positive suggestion has a hypnotic effect which soothes the mind and relaxes you so that you can more readily enter into Rujing. The number of words repeated should be kept to less than ten because the whole phrase has to be repeated slowly in time with the inhalation and exhalation. When there are too many words in the phrase, the breaths and pauses between each breath become overextended to accommodate all the words. This could lead to undesirable side-effects such as headaches, palpitations, and difficulty in breathing. Therefore, just choose a simple phrase with a few key words that mean the most to you.

Another commonly used device for quieting the mind is counting the number of breaths. You can count up to a hundred breaths and start over again when you are finished. This way you can keep your mind occupied and you will gradually enter into Rujing. If you lose count simply start all over again or count to a smaller number like ten and keep repeating this. It is also possible to just concentrate on the sound or feeling of the incoming and outgoing breath without actually counting out each breath. This method requires that your awareness become totally attuned with your breathing. Your awareness should guide your breathing to make it relaxed and slow. Merging your awareness with the ceaseless act of breathing will gradually induce a peaceful state of mind and lead you to the inner calmness of Rujing.

The Meaning of Raising the Tongue

In Inner Regulation Qigong, people are required to raise their tongue to touch the roof of the mouth and then to lower the tongue back down in rhythm with their breathing. In Vitalizing Qigong, the tongue must constantly remain in contact with the roof of the mouth. There is a special reason for raising the tongue in this fashion. It is largely a device to aid concentration and is an important aspect of Qigong along with Diaoshen, Diaoxi, and Diaoxin. Moving the tongue up and down in time with you breathing keeps your mind from becoming distracted by absent thoughts and thus serves as an aid to reaching Rujing.

The up-and-down movement of the tongue also stimulates the region of the cere-brum associated with digestive organs and reflexively influences the digestive function. This causes an increase in the excretion of saliva, and swallowing this saliva while visualizing it reaching Dantain increases your appetite and improves digestion.

The traditional significance of raising the tongue to the hard palate is rooted in a practice of Taoist mystics known as Zhoutian Gong [周天功] (the "circulation of heaven exercise" sometimes referred to as the 'cosmic orbit'"). In this practice those who have reached a certain level of development in Qigong training circulate the Qi energy which has been concentrated at Dantian. First the Qi is guided down to the perineum and then back up the spine to the top of the head and down the middle of the face and the front of the body back down to Dantian. The pathways of energy up and down the vertical centerline of the body on the front and back of the body correspond to the Ren and Du channels of Chinese Medicine. These two channels connect in the mouth when the tip of the tongue is brought in contact with the hard palate. Thus, energy traveling up the spine is able to travel back down the front centerline of the body. This switching point between the two vital channels was called the "bridge of the magpie" by the ancient Chinese, implying a very important link in completing the circulation of Qi in Zhoutian Gong.

This practice of circulating energy should not be pursued by those learning Qigong on their own. The tongue is lightly placed against the roof of the mouth in most Qigong exercises just as a safety precaution. This is to make sure that, in case energy should travel up the spine involuntarily, it will not become trapped in the head. You will notice that placing your tongue on the roof of your mouth has a certain calming effect. You should not force your tongue up against your hard palate because this will cause your tongue to become tired. Further, you should not become preoccupied with your tongue placement or movement because this will detract from breath control and Yishou Dantian and can even lead to uncomfortable sensation in your head. Raising the tongue is always secondary in importance compared with focusing attention on the lower abdomen or your chosen point of concentration.

Basic Guidelines

The following guidelines of Qigong practice are indispensable if you wish to become proficient and obtain good results from the practice of Qigong.

(1)   Relax and stay in a calm and natural state.
It is essential that both the mind and body remain in a relaxed state during the practice of Qigong. The best way to do this is to begin by relaxing your body completely. First, start by loosening all tight clothing as well as belts and straps. You should finish going to the toilet if need be, and make sure that you are completely ready for practice. When assuming the standing or sitting postures for an exercise, try to keep from raising your shoulders or pushing your chest out in an attempt to straighten your back. Never stay in a posture which feels strained or unnatural in any way. If you find that a certain part of your body has become tense or strained during practice, you should try to release this tension and relax this part and return it to a natural state free of tension. It is very important in the practice of Qigong that all the muscles in your body be kept as relaxed as possible. This applies especially to the muscles of the lower abdomen because this is where the circulation of Qi is most vital. Therefore, keep your lower abdomen relaxed and allow it to expand and contract naturally with your breathing.

The next thing is to keep your mind in a peaceful and calm state while practicing

Qigong. Since your attention must be focused on one thing during Qigong exercises, you should not have any preoccupations or distractions. In order to do this, make yourself as calm and relaxed as you can and quietly pay attention to your breathing. Tuning in to the rhythm of your own breathing usually allows you to enter a deep state of mental and physical relaxation. Reaching a calm and relaxed state simply means that you are fully prepared to totally devote your attention to the practice of Qigong and are able to hold down the arousal of your mind to other matters to a bare minimum.

In the state of total relaxation and concentration called Rujing, your sensitivity to external stimulus such as sound and light decreases. In the case of beginners, however, the mind tends to wander during Qigong practice, and such concentration is hard to achieve. When your mind becomes distracted, keep repeating a special phrase of encouragement to yourself such as "I will remain calm and undisturbed" or "My will is firm to overcome this disease" until your mind quiets down. Use of such self-suggestion allows you to attain the state of Rujing comparatively quickly. Nevertheless, it generally takes several months before one is able to reach a state of total relaxation and concentration quickly after beginning to practice, but as long as you are persistent and practice regularly, it is only a matter of time before you will notice definite improvements and come to appreciate the real benefits of Qigong.

(2)   Harmonize the mind and breath.
In Qigong your will (control of mind) and breathing (control of breath) must be harmonized or coordinated as one. Qi or breath can be regulated by your will. You must, therefore, free your mind of distractions and focus your attention on your breathing to regulate its rhythm, speed, and duration. In this way, you must use your conscious will to guide and control your respiration. The key to mind control is to reach a calm and quiet state as explained above. There are seven aspects to breath control which are considered important and these are to breathe long and deep, and to keep your breath slow, thin, and steady, as well as calm and even.

If your breathing becomes quick and shallow or if you become anxious or irritated about something, this is probably caused by improper breathing technique, incorrect posture, or a bad mood unsuitable for practicing Qigong. Also, when you have a headache or feel dizzy before, during, or after practice, this is often caused by forcing the breathing, trying too hard, or by an overactive mind. When such things happen, you should find the cause of the disturbance and correct it so that you can relax and concentrate on your practice.

In Relaxation and Vitalizing Qigong the emphasis is on mind control, whereas in Inner Regulation Qigong the emphasis is on breath control. It should be noted, however, that in all Qigong exercises you must learn to control both your mind and breath so as to harmonize the two. In the beginning, it is hard to keep both the breathing and the object of concentration in your awareness, but once these two elements can be combined into one, your practice of Qigong enters the advanced stage.

(3)   Combine active and passive exercises.

Qigong exercises, because of their quiet nature, tend to be "activity within passivity," as opposed to "passivity within activity" in more vigorous disciplines such as martial arts. That is to say, Qigong is inclined to be a rather sedate form of activity and lacks the salutary effects of vigorous exercises. This is why those who are healthy, as well as those who are ill, must augment Qigong with more active forms of exercise. In this way passive or largely motionless exercises can be combined with appropriate physical activity to yield better results in curing illness, building health, and preventing disease.

Generally, various active exercises are performed after Qigong practice. In China this is referred to as "first passive later active." After finishing a Qigong exercise, it is recommended that you first perform quick and simple self-massage and then go on to practice Tai Chi or some other form of active exercise. Also as another way of "combining active and passive," those who have problems treatable by acupuncture such as neuralgia or low back pain can do some Qigong exercises before receiving a treatment. The effectiveness of acupuncture as well as other types of therapy working with your energy balance is enhanced after once having activated the circulation of Qi (energy) throughout your body. This may be called the "first active and later passive" approach.

(4)   Look for gradual and progressive improvement.

Qigong is a training program for both the mind and body which works within the natural limits of an individual. Being a "training" means that you are able to build up to a certain level of proficiency after repeated practice. No matter how enthusiastic and diligent you may be, it is impossible to attain a high level in a single leap. Save your enthusiasm to practice a little everyday. In this way you will be able to make consistent step-by-step progress to obtain more natural and lasting improvement.

When learning Qigong, you should begin by practicing those postures and breathing techniques which seem easy to you, and as you master these, you can gradually try the more difficult ones. Reaching the state of Rujing is also a cumulative process, which eventually allows you to enter into deep states of relaxation and concentration. Therefore, in the beginning, you should practice for shorter periods in your spare time and gradually work up to longer periods as you become experienced and learn to appreciate the fine points of Qigong. You should remember that in all the aspects of Qigong improvement is a progressive and gradual process which depends more than anything else on the diligence of each individual. Just as it usually takes a long time for a disease to develop, real and lasting improvement never comes overnight.

There are also some general guidelines for ending the practice of Qigong. The first is not to get up and start some activity right after finishing Qigong. Whenever practicing Qigong, it is specially important not to finish abruptly, and for this reason, a series of closing moves should always be performed at the end of the Qigong practice. There are a variety of closing moves designed to facilitate the return to a normal state of activity. The closing moves introduced at the end of the section on Relaxation Qigong are simple and effective for this purpose. In this sequence, you open the eyes and rub the face with both hands and lightly stroke over the eyes.

Next, the back of the neck is massaged and then you get up to lightly exercise the arms and legs. In this manner, you are able to make the gradual and smooth transition from a passive to an active state. This practice is advisable from the standpoint of brain activity. Even after finishing the closing moves, however, you should not begin vigorous or strenuous activity right away because this can sometimes cause uncomfortable sensations in the head.

Another thing which a beginner should be careful about is that you are more prone to catch colds just after practicing Qigong. This is because often you will sweat a little by doing Qigong exercises, and if the temperature is low or there is a draft, this can cause you to become chilled after ending the exercise. After you become proficient in Qigong, however, the resistance of the body will increase to a point where a slight chill or exposure to a draft poses no problem.

Selection of Qigong Exercises

In practicing Qigong, you must select the type of exercise which is most useful and beneficial for your physical condition or ailment. For example, in cases of hypertension, Relaxation Qigong should be the main exercise practiced in the beginning. After a person with hypertension learns this exercise well, he may also practice the Soft Breathing technique of Inner Regulation Qigong. The emphasis on exhalation in this breathing technique will stimulate parasympathetic nerves and have a clear hypotensive effect (lowering of blood pressure).

Inner Regulation Qigong should be practiced in cases of diseases such as pulmonary tuberculosis as well as gastric and duodenal ulcers. Vitalizing Qigong is indicated for cases of neurasthenia. Men who have problems with premature ejaculation and impotence, in addition to practicing Vitalizing Qigong, should perform Preventive Qigong regularly.

When two physical problems such as an ulcer and neurasthenia exist together, the treatment of the acute condition, or the ulcer, comes first. Thus, Inner Regulation Qigong is practiced regularly until the ulcer improves, and if the psychosomatic condition of neurasthenia still remains after this, Vitalizing Qigong is added and performed on alternate days with Inner Regulation Qigong. In cases where Inner Regulation Qigong yields good results for both problems, one only needs to continue this same program. Therefore, when there is more than one physical problem, always address the most serious problem first in your choice of exercises. One exception to this rule is those who are very thin and have a weak constitution. In this case, Inner Regulation Qigong is indicated for all physical problems. Inner Regulation Qigong serves to improve digestion and absorption and effectively strengthens your physical constitution.

Those who are overweight, on the other hand, should practice Vitalizing Qigong or Stepping Qigong instead because these exercises require a comparatively greater expenditure of energy. Those who have weight problems must not practice Inner Regulation Qigong because this can make them gain even more weight.

Where to Practice

One of the most important considerations in the practice of Qigong is to find a suitably quiet and peaceful environment to practice in, whether it is indoors or outdoors. The place of practice is a very important factor for beginners in particular. Quietness of one's surroundings is essential for beginners to attain the state of relaxed concentration known as Rujing. After one has practiced regularly for some time, noise in the surrounding area can be disregarded and the distracting influence of noise can be effectively neutralized. Nevertheless, it does require dedicated practice before people are able to ignore minor disturbances and to retain their composure and concentration. In the beginning, therefore, you must pay special attention to finding a location where you can practice undisturbed.

During Qigong practice, especially when entering Rujing, you should be in an area free of loud voices and big noises because this can have an unsettling influence. Sudden loud noises during Qigong practice can startle and cause "shock waves," which shake people up and destroy their mental composure. In extreme cases, the negative impact is such that a person cannot practice successfully for many days afterward.

Aside from the problem of external disturbances, sometimes people who practice Qigong experience auditory and visual hallucinations. Such noises and sights are not harmful in themselves. As long as you keep your concentration and do not become distracted and do not get caught up in external or internal disturbances, they generally subside of their own accord and pose no problem. If they should occur, exercise your will and keep your concentration to continue practicing so that they pass away by themselves. Such disturbances have an adverse effect only to the extent that you allow them to disrupt your concentration.

Generally the passive variety of Qigong is practiced indoors. There should be good circulation of fresh air and the room should be relatively quiet and be on the dark side. You must be careful, however, not to be exposed to a draft when performing Qigong in the seated or lying postures. Often your body becomes warmed up and sweats a little while practicing Qigong, and exposure to a draft or a slight breeze can cause a cold. In the winter you should either wear plenty of clothes or keep the room temperature fairly high. You can practice Qigong in the lying postures under a light quilt, and if you are practicing in the seated position, you can cover your legs with a blanket.

The active variety of Qigong is most often practiced outdoors early in the morning. Practicing outdoors is preferable when conditions inside are less than ideal and the weather is good. It is best to practice in a park where there are many trees and the air is clean. Find yourself a quiet spot with lots of trees and shrubs and a little privacy. It is also easier to practice as a group in an outdoor setting; so if you wish, you can practice together with some friends.

When and How Much to Practice Qigong

The best time of day to practice Qigong is when you are in the happiest and most relaxed state and when your surroundings are relatively calm and quiet. This could be in the morning before you become involved in the activities of the day, sometimes after taking a nap, in the early evening after work, or before going to bed at night. When you practice at the right time of the day, it is usually much easier to enter the serene state of Rujing and to maintain this state.

For a beginner the length of time for practicing Qigong should be kept between fifteen and twenty minutes. This can gradually be increased to half an hour. The longest practice time should not exceed forty-five minutes. When the practice time is too short, this is not conducive to regulating your breathing and reaching the state of Rujing. Good results cannot be achieved when an adequate amount of time is not set aside for Qigong practice. On the other hand, neither is it good to practice for too long because this could lead to undesirable reactions. The best thing is to allow just enough time to reach a calm and quiet state and slowly go through the exercise. It is not advisable to spend too much time or to make too great an effort in one session.

The amount of practice necessary always depends on the physical condition of the individual as well as his circumstances, such as, work schedule and available free time. You must practice Qigong in a way which fits your own life situation. Those who have serious physical problems and earnestly wish to improve their condition through Qigong should practice four to six times a day for up to one hour at a time. Generally such a person practices once upon waking, and once or twice in the morning and in the afternoon, and then once before retiring at night. If a person is hospitalized, a minimum of four times a day for one hour at a time is necessary to obtain significant improvement.

Those who are partially disabled and work half days should practice Qigong three or four times a day. This could be done once upon waking, once or twice during the day, and once before retiring. Those who are not ill and work full days and desire to improve their physical condition should practice two or three times a day utilizing spare time in the morning, noon, and evening. They can practice thirty minutes to an hour each time.

The majority of people who practice Qigong either have only minor physical problems or are perfectly healthy. Thus, most people practice Qigong for the purpose of prevention, enhancement of health, and longevity. Practicing Qigong once or twice a day for thirty minutes to an hour is sufficient for this purpose. It must be emphasized, however, that regular practice is essential if you wish to obtain the full benefits of Qigong.

The ideal amount of time for practice also depends on the type of Qigong being practiced. Medical Qigong and Qigong for Health are each practiced for different amounts of time. Medical Qigong, during a period of convalescence in a hospital or at home, is generally practiced three to four times a day for half an hour at a time. If one is recovering from an illness while continuing to work, once or twice a day for half an hour at a time is sufficient. In the case of Qigong for Health, once a day or once every other day for thirty to forty-five minutes is adequate.

When Not to Practice Qigong

There are times when practicing Qigong can be counterproductive and even harmful. One should learn the undesirable conditions before attempting to begin the practice of Qigong.

(1)   On a full or a very empty stomach
Practicing Qigong on a full stomach poses a problem because the expanded condition of the stomach makes it difficult to breathe deeply. It is best to wait at least half an hour after a meal before beginning the practice of Qigong. Conversely, when practicing Qigong on a very empty stomach, the peristaltic action of the intestines can become too strong. This can cause a person to feel even greater hunger, which is distracting and not conducive to the state of Rujing.

(2)   Excessively fatigued condition
When people who are very tired try to practice passive Qigong, the usual result is that they fall asleep. Therefore, it is best to practice Qigong when you feel well rested. Nevertheless, when you are just a little tired, Qigong has a refreshing effect on the mind and helps you to recover from fatigue. Relaxation Qigong or Vitalizing Qigong is recommended for this purpose. In this case, the practice time should be shortened slightly because practicing too long could have the opposite of the desired effect.

(3)   Excited or irritated states
In a situation where you are in a hurry or anxious, such as, when you are trying to make it on time to work, it is best not to practice Qigong. Also you should put off the practice of Qigong when there is something which is irritating or otherwise bothering you. The main reason Qigong is not recommended when you are in these states is because you will not be able to do the exercises correctly with other over-riding concerns on your mind. Nevertheless, since Qigong can be helpful in calming you down, if you are feeling a little bit tense or nervous and are not pressed for time, you may practice Relaxation Qigong. This should allow you to relax and calm down as long as the problem is not serious.

(4)   Other abnormal conditions
Aside from the above mentioned conditions, when one has a high fever, severe diarrhea, or a bad cold, it is best not to practice Qigong for a while. Although women can continue practicing Qigong through their menstrual period, they should take care to never strain themselves during any of the exercises. If menstrual cramps should occur during practice, they should quit practicing immediately.

Chapter 3

Qigong Practices

Relaxation Qigong 放鬆功

The Effects

Relaxation Qigong is a Qigong exercise for progressive relaxation in which the whole body is gradually brought to a state of total relaxation. After you become proficient at this exercise, not only will you be able to completely relax your body at will, but you will also be able to make your mind calm and relaxed. Among all the Qigong exercises, this relaxation exercise is one of the simplest and easiest to practice. It can be called the foundation for all other Qigong exercises, and it is often used as the preliminary step in beginning other Qigong exercises.

Relaxation Qigong is the first exercise taught to beginners in the Shanghai Qigong Therapy Institute. This exercise is usually the very first thing taught in Qigong because, in addition to relaxation being essential in Qigong, learning to relax all the muscles and joints in the body serves to prevent distracting reactions in Qigong such as involuntary movements in limbs, which occur more often in beginners.

Relaxation Qigong has a profound effect in relieving stress and fatigue. It is therefore very useful for improving your health and preventing disease. It is the most fundamental step in all Qigong exercises, and success with this exercise directly relates to relief from stress related condition such as hypertension, gastric ulcers, insomnia, indigestion, and constipation.

How to Practice

The practice of Relaxation Qigong is based on the following four principles or steps.
    (1)   Diaoshen (prepare posture)—Assume correct posture
    (2)   Diaoxi (regulate breath)—Control breathing
    (3)   Yishou (hold attention)—Keep attention focused
    (4)   Closing Moves
Each of these steps in Relaxation Qigong is explained in sequence below.

(1)   Diaoshen (prepare posture)
1. Lie in a supine position with your head raised slightly higher than your feet. If you lie on the floor you can place some pillows or blankets under your head and shoulders to assume this reclined position.
2. If lying on a bed, place pillows under your head to raise it about ten inches and

also support your back with some blankets or a quilt to keep your back comfortable and straight.

3. After lying down on your back, draw your chin slightly in and straighten out your body. Your arms should rest comfortably at your side with the palms facing down and your fingers spread apart comfortably. Your legs should be stretched straight out in a relaxed and natural manner (Fig. 1).

4. Gently close your eyes.

5. Keep your mouth closed with your jaws relaxed so your upper and lower teeth are barely touching and touch the roof of your mouth lightly with the tip of your tongue.

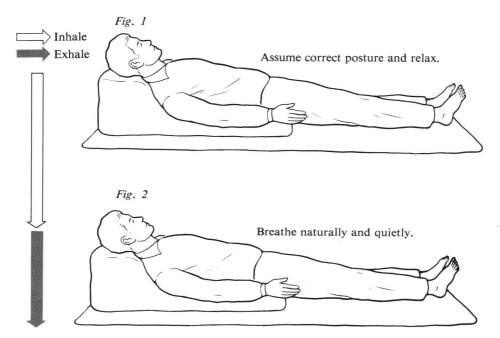

Fig. 1

Inhale
Exhale

Assume correct posture and relax.

Fig. 2

Breathe naturally and quietly.

(2) Diaoxi (regulate breath)

1. Breathe naturally through your nose (Fig. 2).

2. Continue breathing in and out naturally through your nose. This breathing does not have to be any deeper than normal, but you should try to keep it relatively thin (so that the breathing is not audible), smooth and steady.

(3) Yishou (hold attention)

This is the last and most important step in Relaxation Qigong, where you relax different parts of your body successively with each breath. Hold your attention on one part of your body as you inhale and allow this part to relax as you exhale. Start with your head and work down to your toes with each successive breath to relax your body from head to toe. As you become used to this, you should experience this as warm waves of relaxation flowing down your body.

1. Focus your attention on your head as you inhale (Fig. 3).

2. Think "relax" to yourself as you exhale and feel how your head becomes light and relaxed (Fig. 4).

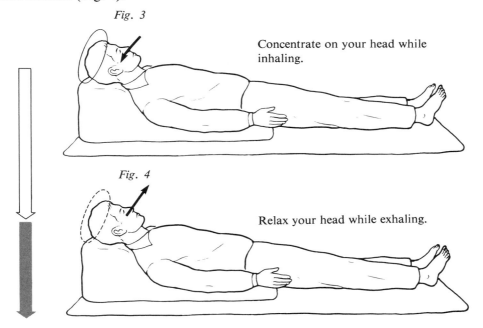

Fig. 3

Concentrate on your head while inhaling.

Fig. 4

Relax your head while exhaling.

3. As you inhale again shift your attention to your shoulders (Fig. 5).

4. Think "relax" to yourself as you exhale and feel how both shoulders become relaxed (Fig. 6).

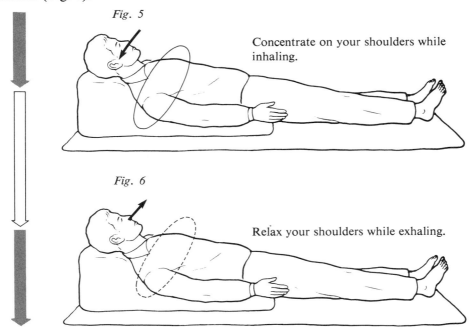

Fig. 5

Concentrate on your shoulders while inhaling.

Fig. 6

Relax your shoulders while exhaling.

5. Proceed in this way to progressively relax each part of you body in the following sequence.

arms ⟶ hands ⟶ chest ⟶ stomach ⟶
back ⟶ hips ⟶ thighs ⟶ calves ⟶ feet

After relaxing all the muscles in your body in this way, you can go on to relax all your blood vessels, nerves, and internal organs by the same method. The aim is to release residual tension in all parts of your body to bring total relaxation over your whole body.

(4)   Closing moves
Do not stand up all of a sudden after you are finished with this relaxation exercise. The closing moves below are used to smooth the transition from a passive state to an active state. Always perform some closing moves before ending a Qigong practice session.
1.   Slowly open your eyes and place the palms of your hands on your forehead (Fig. 7).
2.   Close your eyes as you gently rub over your face with the palms of your hands (Fig. 8).

Fig. 7   *Fig. 8*

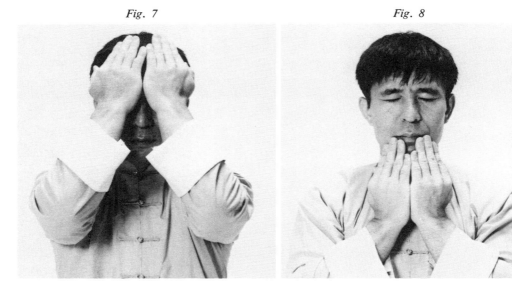

3.   Massage the back of your neck thoroughly, using both hands (Figs. 9 and 10).
4.   Stand up slowly.
5.   Shift your weight onto one leg and briskly move your arms and leg back and forth to cause a shaking motion (Fig. 11).
6.   Stand up on your toes and then drop back down onto your heels. Repeat this movement several times up to twenty times (Figs. 12 and 13).

49

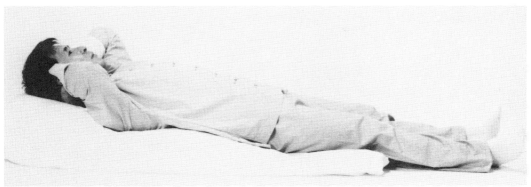

Fig. 9   Fig. 10

The above movements serve to activate circulation all over the body. Your choice of Preventive Qigong (self-administered massage) techniques introduced later can be substituted for these closing moves. You can resume normal activities indoors or outdoors after completing a sequence of closing moves.

Fig. 11   Fig. 12   Fig. 13

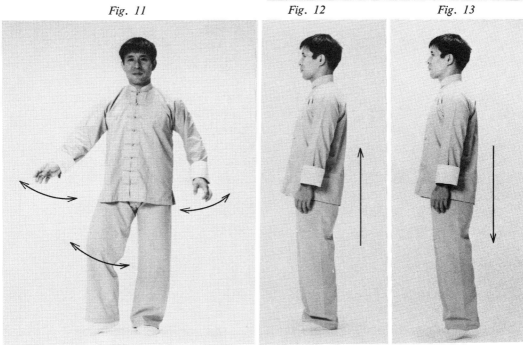

How Much to Practice

The right amount of practice always depends on your physical condition. When hospitalized or recuperating at home, three to four times a day for thirty minutes at a time is best. When one is working half-days, or otherwise working a full day after recovering from a illness, once a day or twice a day for thirty minutes at a time is sufficient.

There is no set duration or number of days which Relaxation Qigong should be practiced. Generally, however, you should keep practicing with the understanding that it takes two or three months of regular practice before lasting benefits can be realized.

Inner Regulation Qigong　內養功

The Effects

Inner Regulation Qigong, which belongs to the Passive Qigong category, is one of the main Qigong exercises. Historically, this method of Qigong was orally transmitted in China from one generation to the next by a Qigong master teaching only his best disciple. This secret method for health and longevity was first made available to the public in 1947 after Dr. Liu Gui-zhen, with the help of his associates Li Wei-hua and Chang You-tian, persuaded Liu Du-zhou, a Qigong master from the Hebei Province, to reveal his secret. After reorganizing these secret practices into a simpler formula, Dr. Liu began teaching this simplified method to patients in hospitals and found that his formula had a remarkable therapeutic effect. He published his findings and popularized this method as Neiyanggong [內養功], or Inner Regulation Qigong. It has since become one of the most basic approaches among the many varieties of Passive Qigong.

The main feature of Inner Regulation Qigong is that brain activity is slowed down while the function of internal organs are heightened by placing emphasis on silently repeating a phrase to yourself and concentrating on the Dantian point (lower abdomen). Since this Qigong exercise strengthens the internal organs, it has a very marked effect in curing or preventing diseases of the digestive system such as ulcers, gastroptosis, and chronic constipation, in addition to diseases of the respiratory system. Also, this Qigong exercise is widely practiced because it is known to have a remarkable effect in improving people's physical constitution and prolonging life.

How to Practice

The practice of Inner Regulation Qigong is based on the following five principles or steps.
   (1)   Relaxation—Completely relax mind and body
   (2)   Diaoshen (prepare posture)—Assume correct posture

(3)   Repeat Phrase—Silently repeat a special phrase
(4)   Diaoxi (regulate breath)—Control breathing
(5)   Yishou (hold attention)—Keep attention focused
Each of these steps of Inner Regulation Qigong will be explained in sequence.

(1)   Relaxation

One of the keys to success in practicing any Qigong exercise is to know how to fully prepare yourself for an exercise, and another important thing is to know how to keep your mind and body completely relaxed throughout the period of practice. As stated earlier, relaxation involves the two aspects of mind and body, and the body must be put at ease before the mind is able to relax completely. Drink enough water before practice so that you do not have a thirst, and otherwise go to the restroom if necessary before starting. Those wearing a hat or glasses should remove these. Undo all buttons of tight fitting clothing as well as belts and watch bands and shoe strings (remove your shoes where possible). Start relaxing all the muscles in your body progressively from your head to your toes until you are completely relaxed. After relaxing your body completely, you should set aside all other concerns so as to prepare yourself for Qigong practice. Being in a calm and cheerful mood is essential to achieving the proper degree of concentration. Refer to the previous section on Relaxation Qigong for more detail on how to relax mentally and physically.

(2)   Diaoshen (prepare posture)

There are four basic positions in Inner Regulation Qigong and they are the side-lying, supine, seated, and reclining positions. These will each be explained individually.

Side-lying position: Lie on your side on the floor or a bed. When lying on a bed, the bed should not be too soft. If the temperature is low, you can place a blanket or light quilt over yourself. Adjust the position of your head with a pillow so that it stays straight and in line with your spine. If anything, your head should be tilted slightly forward toward your chest. Straighten and expand your back and bring your chest just slightly in so that you are able to assume the so-called "contained chest spread back" posture. This is simply an expression for keeping your chest drawn in slightly while keeping your back straight. There is no need to become tense trying to get in this posture. Just straighten your back and keep your chest slightly to the inside in a relaxed and comfortable fashion.

   When lying on your right side, your right arm should be bent at the elbow to place your right hand on the pillow about two inches from your face with the palm facing up. Your left arm should be comfortably straight and your left hand should be placed on the side of your hip with the palm down. Your right leg should just be kept comfortable and straight, and your left leg should be bent at the knee at around an 120 degree angle so that one knee is placed on the other and the left foot goes to the back. When lying on your left side, you should assume the same posture but reverse the position of the limbs on the right and left.

   After you have assumed a comfortable and stable position, close both of your eyes or leave them just barely open so you can only see one thin streak of light. In this case, fix your gaze on either your nose or your feet. Close your mouth or leave it open slightly according to the breathing method (Fig. 14).

Fig. 14

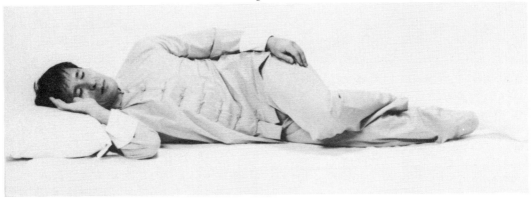

Supine position: Lie flat on your back on a bed or on the floor. Draw your chin in just a little and straighten you body out. Your arms should rest at your sides with your palms facing down and fingers comfortably spread out. Your legs should be stretched straight out in a natural manner with your heels together and the toes pointing comfortably outward. Your eyes and your mouth should be the same as in the side-lying position (Fig. 15).

Fig. 15

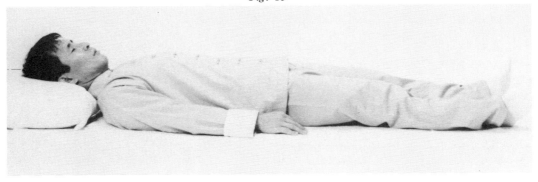

Seated position (with seat): Sit on a chair or stool with your back straight. Tilt your head slightly forward and assume the "contained chest" posture. Relax your shoulders and let your elbows hang loosely. Place your hands, palms down, on your thighs with the fingers comfortably loose. Place your feet parallel to each other on the floor about shoulder-width apart. Your knees should be bent at a right angle so your thighs are parallel with the floor. When your chair is not high enough for this, place a blanket on the chair to increase the height, and when it is too high,

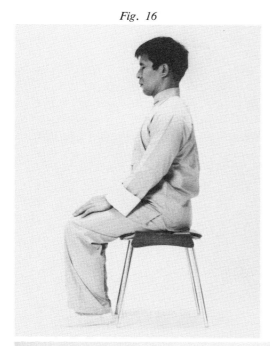

Fig. 16

place something under your feet to get in the right position. Your eyes and mouth should be the same as in the side-lying position (Fig. 16).

Reclining position: Assume the same reclining position that was explained in the section for Relaxation Qigong (Fig. 17).

The position that is recommended for beginners among the above four positions is either the supine position or the side-lying position. You should choose the lying posture that seems most suitable or comfortable to you, taking into consideration your physical condition. The side-lying position with the right side

Fig. 17

down is the best for those with weak stomachs because this position facilitates the passage of food from the stomach to the intestines. This position is also recommended for times when you practice soon after eating. People with pyloric prolapse, however, should avoid using this position because the pull of gravity on the stomach lining can aggravate the prolapse.

Able bodied people can practice Qigong exclusively in the seated position, and otherwise it can be used from time to time alternating with lying postures. The advantage of this seated position is that it is harder to fall asleep and easier to concentrate. The reclining position is best used in Qigong for relaxing and increasing vitality and is often used at the beginning or at the end of Qigong practice. Those who are bed-ridden can use one of the lying positions, and once they recover, they can switch to the seated position.

(3)   Repeat phrase

In order to keep your mind on Diaoxi (regulate breath), the device of repeating a special phrase to yourself is used. You must repeat a special phrase over and over inside your mind. You must not vocalize this phrase. In China people generally start with a phrase with three characters or words. The number of words can be increased according to the effect desired, but people in China are discouraged from having more than nine words in their phrase. It is best for the phrase to be short and to the point. The words used are usually those suggesting relaxation, beauty, and health. Some examples of phrases used in China are as follows;

"I am calm."
"I sit calmly."
"I sit calmly and my body is well."
"I sit calmly and I become healthy."
"My whole body is relaxed."
"My mind is at rest and my organs are working."
"Daily practice builds my health."

Special phrases like those listed above must be worked in with the Dioaxi, or breath control, which will be explained next. Your breathing must be in perfect synchronization with each repetition of the phrase. For example, when repeating the phrase "I am calm," the word "I" is imagined while inhaling and "am" is imagined while pausing between the inhalation and exhalation and "calm" is imagined while exhaling. The phrase thereby serves to focus your mind and remove distracting thoughts.

The thing which needs to be emphasized here is that although the words in the special phrase must be distributed evenly during the breathing, they are not meant to change the speed or length of the inhalation, exhalation, or the pause between breaths. There is no set time in which one word must be covered. This is entirely up to each person. The phrase should be kept short and simple to avoid getting it mixed up during practice.

The self-suggestion of these phrases are used to obtain corresponding physiological effects. Therefore, the wording of the special phrase should be tailored to the circumstances of each individual. Those who tend to get nervous and tense should repeat "I am relaxed." Those with poor digestion should repeat "My mind is at rest and my organs are working." Those who have a sensation of discomfort or obstruction in their chest should repeat "My energy is concentrated in my lower abdomen."

Since the phrases listed above were obtained from Chinese texts, they need to be modified somewhat for English speaking people. The phrase "I am calm and relaxed" is a good one for beginners. This phrase will be the one used for explaining the breathing techniques which follow. You can go on to create your own special phrase which has the most meaning for you. Original phrases are just as effective so long as the words are repeated in rhythm with your breathing.

(4)   Diaoxi (regulate breath)

The breathing techniques in Inner Regulation Qigong are one of the main features of these Qigong exercises, and it is essential that these techniques of diaphragmatic breathing be practiced and mastered. Diaphragmatic breathing simply means to allow your abdomen to expand gradually and fully as you inhale and to let it return to normal as you exhale. The objective here is to obtain distinct expansion and contraction movements in the abdominal wall with each breath. The breathing techniques in Inner Regulation Qigong are a little complicated because the four aspects of breathing, pauses between breaths, tongue movement, and repetition of a special phrase need to be combined. There are actually three breathing techniques that are used in Inner Regulation Qigong, but only the most commonly used techniques of Soft Breathing and Hard Breathing will be explained in this book.

Soft Breathing is suited to those with illnesses or those in poor physical condition as well as those who are beginners at Qigong. This breathing technique is specially beneficial for those who have respiratory ailments or those whose breathing is shallow and irregular. Hard Breathing should be practiced by those of middle age or younger and by those who have no serious illness and are in comparatively good physical condition. This breathing technique has a powerful effect for increasing stamina. *People with high blood pressure must not practice Hard Breathing.* Also it should be noted that the Soft and Hard Breathing Techniques are not to be practiced alternately or in combination with each other. You must decide which technique is most suited to your condition and stick to this technique.

Soft Breathing Technique

Soft Breathing Technique is for those who are beginners to Qigong, those who are in a rather weak condition, and those with respiratory problems. In order to make things simple, just the breathing technique will be presented first, and the special phrase will be combined after this. Always begin with step one (relaxation) and step two (Diaoshen) before beginning the breathing technique. Once you are ready, close your mouth lightly and touch the tip of your tongue on the roof of your mouth.

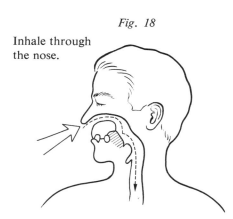

Fig. 18

Inhale through the nose.

1.   Slowly inhale through your nose and imagine that your breath is being drawn down into you lower abdomen. This is important for the next step of concentrating on "Dantian," the point below the navel. Your lower abdomen should fill out naturally in this process. Be careful not to inhale too deeply or to strain yourself when you do this (Fig. 18).

2.   Let your tongue down and open your mouth slightly and exhale slowly. You can exhale through your nose and your mouth simultaneously. Your lower abdomen should go in naturally (Fig. 19).

56

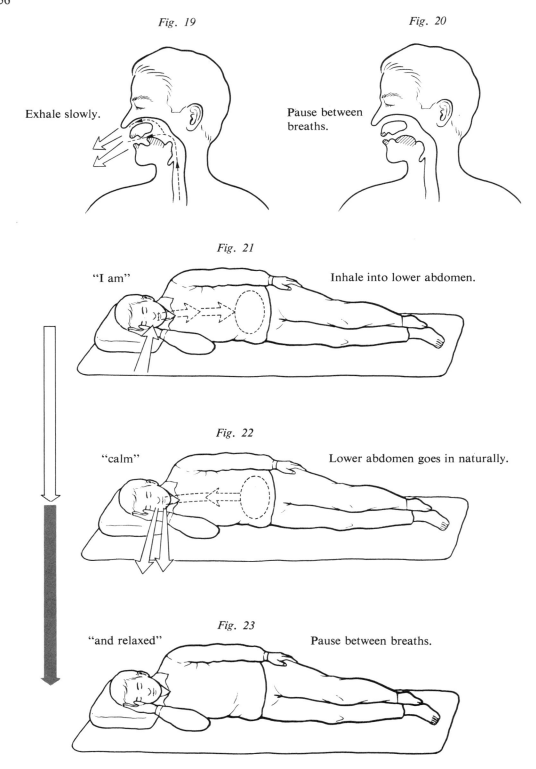

Fig. 19

Exhale slowly.

Fig. 20

Pause between breaths.

Fig. 21

"I am"

Inhale into lower abdomen.

Fig. 22

"calm"

Lower abdomen goes in naturally.

Fig. 23

"and relaxed"

Pause between breaths.

3. After exhaling completely, let your breathing pause briefly in a natural way. Leave your tongue down and your mouth slightly open. Your abdomen should also remain slightly collapsed (Fig. 20).

The main points of this breathing technique are to slowly inhale through the nose, exhale through the nose and mouth, and to pause momentarily before inhaling through the nose again. Once you become used to this method of breathing, begin practicing it while repeating your special phrase. Just silently repeat the phrase to yourself in time with your breathing and the movement of your mouth and tongue. This breathing technique is combined with the special phrase as follows:

1. Close your mouth lightly and touch the tip of your tongue on the roof of your mouth and slowly inhale through your nose. While breathing in, feel your breath being drawn down into your lower abdomen and think to yourself "I am" (Fig. 21).

2. Let your tongue down and open your mouth slightly. Exhale slowly and allow your abdomen to go in naturally as you think the word "calm" (Fig. 22).

3. After exhaling completely, let your breathing pause naturally and keep your mouth and tongue as well as your lower abdomen relaxed and in the same position. Think the words "and relaxed" while your breathing is paused momentarily (Fig. 23).

Continue breathing and repeating your special phrase in this way for the duration of your practice period. When finishing this breathing exercise, be sure to end with the closing moves introduced previously with Relaxation Qigong.

Hard Breathing Technique

Hard Breathing Technique is for those who are in relatively good physical condition. This method of breathing is sometimes a little difficult for beginners, so begin by practicing just the breathing. First complete step one (relaxation) and step two (Diaoshen) before beginning this breathing technique. Once you are ready, close your mouth lightly and touch the tip of your tongue on the roof of your mouth.

1. Slowly inhale through your nose and imagine that your breath is being drawn down into you lower abdomen. Drawing your breath into your lower abdomen is

Fig. 24

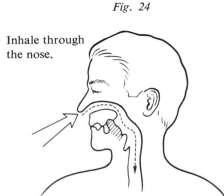

Inhale through the nose.

essential for the next step of concentrating on "Dantian," the point below the navel. Be careful not to inhale too deeply or to strain yourself in an attempt to do this. Just relax and allow your mind to guide your breath downward (Fig. 24).

2. After inhaling, pause your breath briefly while keeping your tongue in the same position, touching the roof of your mouth. Keep your lower abdomen expanded. Pause only as long as comfortable. Never strain yourself to hold your breath (Fig. 25).

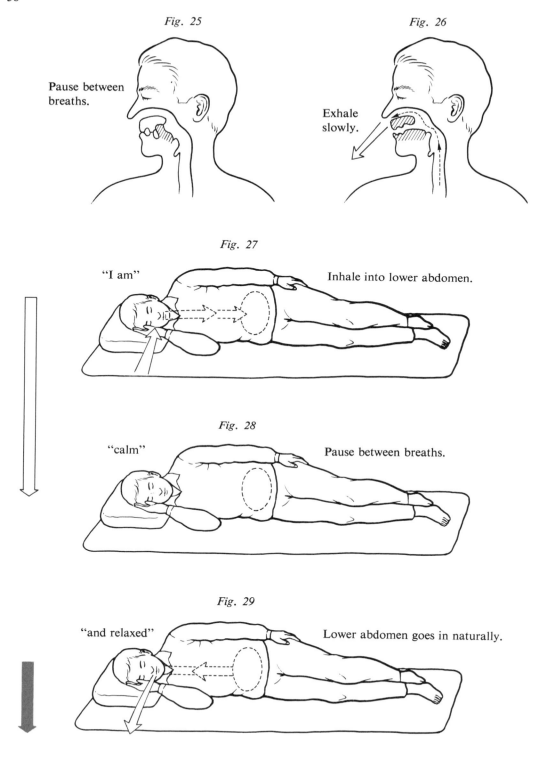

Fig. 25

Pause between breaths.

Fig. 26

Exhale slowly.

Fig. 27

"I am"

Inhale into lower abdomen.

Fig. 28

"calm"

Pause between breaths.

Fig. 29

"and relaxed"

Lower abdomen goes in naturally.

3. Let your tongue down and exhale slowly through your nose, allowing your lower abdomen to go back in naturally in the process (Fig. 26).

The main points of this breathing technique are to breathe repeatedly through the nose inhaling slowly, pausing momentarily, and then exhaling slowly each time. Once you become used to this way of breathing, begin practicing this technique together with your special phrase. The words of your phrase must be repeated silently in time with your breathing and tongue movement. This breathing technique and the special phrase should be combined as follows:

1. Close your mouth lightly and touch the tip of your tongue on the roof of your mouth and inhale through your nose. At the same time imagine this breath being drawn down to your lower abdomen. As your lower abdomen begins to fill out naturally, silently imagine the words "I am" (Fig. 27).

2. Keep your tongue in place and pause your breathing briefly, keeping your abdomen expanded, and silently think the word "calm" as you do this (Fig. 28).

3. After a short pause, let your tongue down and exhale through your nose slowly while thinking the words "and relaxed" (Fig. 29).

Just keep breathing this way and repeating your special phrase for the duration of your practice period. When finishing this breathing exercise, be sure to end with the closing moves introduced previously with Relaxation Qigong.

(5) Yishou (hold attention)

No matter whether you choose to practice Soft Breathing or Hard Breathing of Inner Regulation Qigong, after you reach a level of proficiency where these breathing exercises can be practiced for up to a half an hour without effort, you are ready to go onto the next step of Yishou. Once you become practiced at Yishou, you will be able to enter the totally calm state of Rujing at will. Nevertheless, it is not so easy to perform the breathing technique, phrase repetition, and Yishou all together at the same time. Therefore, in order not to "fall between two stools," so to speak, it is important that you begin practicing Yishou techniques only after you have mastered and gained confidence in either the Soft Breathing or Hard Breathing Techniques.

Yishou [意守] means to keep one's attention focused on some object or mental image. Yishou is a technique for mental concentration, which allows one to dispell distracting thoughts, and it is one of the most important steps in the practice of Qigong. The three most common Yishou techniques used in Inner Regulation Qigong are Yishou Dantian [意守丹田], Yishou Shanzhong [意守膻中], and Yishou Jiaozhi [意守脚趾] (see Fig. 30). In all of these Yishou techniques one's attention is focused on a particular point on the body. Among these three methods, Yishou Dantian is by far the most often used. The reason that Yishou Dantian is the most widely practiced method is because it is the most reliable and time tested method of concentration. Yishou Dantian serves to harmonize the energy and physiological activity in the head, chest, and abdomen. Yishou Dantian is also the easiest method for keeping one's attention focused while coordinating the silent repetition of a phrase and one's breathing along with the expansion and contraction of the abdomen. Good

Fig. 30

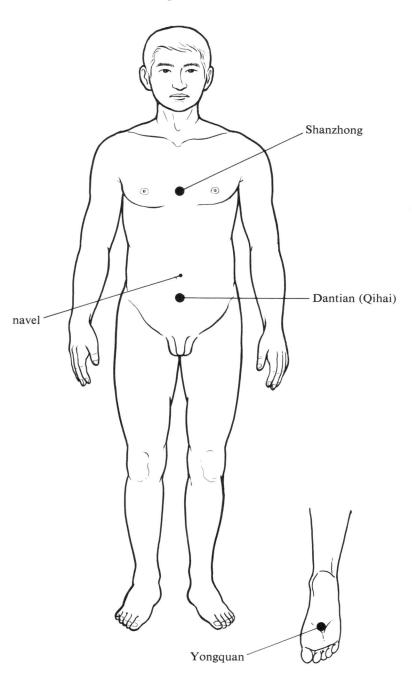

Shanzhong

Dantian (Qihai)

navel

Yongquan

timing induces a relaxed state of concentration which reduces mental distractions so that Rujing can be attained with comparative ease.

In the case of women, however, there are times when Yishou Dantian lengthens the period of menstruation or otherwise causes excessive menstrual discharge. If this happens, they should immediately switch to Yishou Shanzhong. Otherwise, those who find it difficult to stop incessant thoughts from coming up in their minds usually have a hard time concentrating on the Dantian point, so these people should switch to Yishou Jiaozhi and concentrate on their feet.

No matter where you decide to focus your attention, or which Yishou technique you adopt, it is important that you do this in a natural and relaxed manner. Only continue practicing Yishou as long as you are comfortable doing it. The three most commonly practiced Yishou techniques are explained below. You should practice the one which suits you the most and stick with it. Combine this Yishou technique, or method of concentration, with your practice of either the Soft or Hard Breathing of Inner Regulation Qigong. Keep practicing regularly with the aim of reaching the state of Rujing.

Yishou Dantian: Yishou Dantian is the most reliable and widely used Yishou technique as just stated. Dantian (pronounced Dantien) is a term which comes up repeatedly in Qigong, and it is fundamental concept in all Oriental practices for health. In Japan, this center of energy is referred to as *tanden* or *hara*. As with any important and profound concept, there are various viewpoints regarding Dantian. For the purpose of Inner Regulation Qigong, however, Dantian is just a place about four centimeters (around 1½ inches) below the navel. This corresponds to the acupuncture point Qihai (pronounced Cheehai), which means the sea of Qi. Traditionally this was regarded as the point where Qi originated and where Qi collected. It has even been said that learning to concentrate on this one point keeps a person robust and energetic and that one can cure all types of diseases this way.

Although the Dantian corresponds to an acupuncture point, there is no need to be too concerned about its exact location. All that is necessary is that you are able to visualize your center of energy as being just below your navel. When you concentrate on Dantian, just visualize a small area below your navel around the Qihai point. You can also imagine a small ball or sphere of energy just beneath the skin at this point. The main thing is that you keep your attention focused on this area below your navel in a relaxed manner.

Yishou Shanzhong: Yishou Shanzhong is particularly suited to women. Shanzhong (pronounced Shanjong) is an acupuncture point located in the middle of the breast-bone (sternum) directly between the two nipples. Shanzhong is regarded as the energy center for the heart, which in traditional Chinese medicine is considered to house the mind. Again, there is no need to be too concerned about the exact location of this point. Simply visualize a point in the center of the chest and concentrate on this. Find the point in the center of your chest which is the easiest to concentrate on for you. This can be as low as the bottom of the breastbone.

Yishou Jiaozhi: Yishou Jiaozhi is most suited to those who find it difficult to concentrate. The eyes are left barely open to admit a thin streak of light, and the line of vision is directed to the tip of the big toes. Do not try to look at your feet as such, but instead just visualize your feet and keep your awareness focused on them. You may choose to focus your awareness on the acupuncture point Yongquan (pronounced Yungchuan) on the soles of your feet. Yongquan is located at the center of the sole just behind the ball of the foot, but once again, there is no need to become overly concerned with the precise location. Just keep your attention fixed on the center of your soles.

How Much to Praction

Those who are ill should refer to the section on Qigong for different diseases. Those who just have a generally weak physical constitution or those who are basically healthy and are practicing Qigong for general health, prevention of disease, and longevity should practice once or twice a day. The ideal way to practice is to do thirty minutes to one hour early in the morning and/or before going to bed at night. Beginners should not practice for long periods. It is best to gradually lengthen the practice time as you become more experienced.

Vitalizing Qigong 強壯功

The Effects

Vitalizing Qigong is an exercise which was created by distilling the essence of Buddhist, Taoist, and Confucian meditation exercises and combining them with elements from other mystical practices originating in China. This exercise has been shown to be effective in treating circulatory disorders such as hypertension and heart disease, respiratory diseases such as asthma, and nervous conditions such as neurosis. Vitalizing Qigong is very effective for improving the physical constitution of people who are ill, and it also increases the level of health and resistance to disease for people who are already healthy. Vitalizing Qigong is widely practiced among the elderly in China for staying robust and healthy in their old age because it strengthens one's life-force when practiced regularly.

How to Practice

Vitalizing Qigong is simpler than Inner Regulation Qigong because there is no need to silently repeat a phrase and the breathing technique is easier. Therefore, those who have practiced Inner Regulation Qigong usually have no trouble with this exercise and learn it very quickly. The basic steps in Vitalizing Qigong are as follows:
   (1)   Relaxation—Completely relax the mind and body

(2) Diaoshen (adjust posture)—Assume correct posture

(3) Diaoxi (regulate breath)—Control breathing

(4) Yishou (hold attention)—Keep attention focused

Each of these steps will be explained in order, but since the first step of relaxing the mind and body is exactly the same as that for Inner Regulation Qigong, this will be omitted. Refer back to Inner Regulation Qigong section for details on how to relax mentally and physically.

Fig. 31

Fig. 32

(2) Diaoshen (adjust posture)

There are five basic positions that are used in Vitalizing Qigong and three of these are the seated postures of the cross-legged position, the half lotus position, and the full lotus position; the other two postures are the standing position and the free position. How to assume each of these postures will be explained in detail, beginning with the seated postures.

Cross-legged position: Sit down with both legs crossed so the soles of your feet face outward in a comfortable cross-legged fashion. Keep your head, neck, and back straight in line and draw your hips back slightly. Expand your back and bring your chest in slightly to assume the contained chest posture. Then relax your neck muscles so that your head tilts slightly forward. Lightly close your eyes and mouth. Place both arms on your lap in front of your lower abdomen with the palms facing up. You may either hold one hand lightly in the other or just place one hand over the other. The main point is to keep your shoulders, arms, and hands completely relaxed (Fig. 31).

Half lotus position: Sit down with both legs crossed and place the right foot over the left thigh so the sole of the right foot faces up. The reverse of this, with the left foot placed over the right thigh, is just as good. Choose whichever position that is most comfortable and easy to maintain. Keep your spine straight and relax your shoulders and arms completely. The hands are placed in the lap right in front of the lower abdomen just as in the cross-legged position (Fig. 32).

Full lotus position: Sit down cross-legged and place your right foot on your left thigh. Then bring your left foot over your right calf and place it on your right thigh so that both soles face up. The reverse of this, with the right leg over the left, is just as good; choose the position which suits you the best. Keep the spine straight and relax your shoulders and arms completely. The hands are placed in the same manner as the cross-legged position (Fig. 33).

Fig. 33

Fig. 34

Fig. 35

Standing position: Stand with your feet apart about shoulder-width. Bend your knees just slightly and straighten your back while keeping your chest "contained." Tilt your head forward just a little and close your eyes lightly. Relax your shoulders and let your arms hang loosely by your side. Then bend your elbows slightly, like your knees, and hold your hands in front of your lower abdomen as if you were holding a large ball with your arms and hands. It is also possible to raise both arms up with the elbows comfortably bent so the arms are close to horizontal. You can hold your open hands out in front of your chest to form a large circle with your chest and extended arms. The arm position depends on where you intend to concentrate: If you concentrate on Dantian, the former position is better; if you concentrate on Shanzhong the latter position is better. In either position you must hold your hands several inches apart and keep your shoulders and arms as relaxed as possible (Figs. 34 and 35).

Free position: Vitalizing Qigong can actually be practiced in any posture as long as a few basic requirements are met. The requirements are that you relax your whole body, keep your spine straight, and breathe deeply so that you are able to concentrate on your Dantian point. It is also necessary that you are able to maintain this position comfortably for a certain length of time and avoid the unnecessary interruption of changing your posture during the practice. Sitting on a chair is ideal because it is not very tiring, but you can choose any posture, standing or sitting, that feels right for you.

In this way, you can practice Vitalizing Qigong anytime and anywhere. It is very effective for times when you have become a little tired at work or when you feel the need to relax after having been preoccupied with something. You will be able to recover from fatigue very quickly once you learn to release your stress this way, and brief Qigong sessions like this will prevent the accumulation of fatigue, raise your work efficiency, and increase your overall level of health and well-being.

Those who are in a weakened physical condition should start practicing in either one of the lying positions or seated positions. These people can change to the standing position after practicing Qigong for a long time and gaining confidence. Those who have no physical problems can choose any position they like.

For the sake of convenience, the cross-legged position will be used in the explanations of this section on how to practice Vitalizing Qigong.

(3) Diaoxi (regulate breath)

There are three options for the breathing technique used in the practice of Vitalizing Qigong: They are Quiet Breathing, Deep Breathing, and Inverse Breathing. These breathing techniques are similar to those used in Inner Regulation Qigong. That is, you breathe through the nostrils and raise the tongue to touch the hard palate. When you have nasal congestion and your nose is not clear, the mouth can be opened a little so that you may breathe more easily. The Quiet Breathing technique can be used any time, but Deep Breathing and Inverse Breathing must not be practiced right after a meal.

Quiet Breathing simply means natural breathing. Instead of trying to control your respiration in any way, you should just breathe naturally. This natural breathing is most suited to older people and those who have respiratory problems or those who are physically weak.

In Deep Breathing, your breath is made progressively deeper and longer in duration. While you inhale, your chest and abdomen should slowly expand in unison. The more you practice, the more you should be able to make your breathing long, thin, and even. This way of breathing is suited to those who have problems with neurasthenia or constipation and also people who have difficulty in concentrating.

In Inverse Breathing you expand the chest while inhaling and simultaneously contract the lower abdomen. Conversely, while exhaling, the chest is compressed and the lower abdomen is expanded. This method of breathing should be practiced cautiously at first so that you do not hyperventilate. You must not become too anxious to make progress and strain or overdo this breathing method because this technique, more than others, needs to be mastered in stages. With some practice, you will reach a point where the expanding and contracting movements in the abdominal wall come with ease in a relaxed fashion along with deep and slow breathing. Inverse Breathing increases physical energy when practiced correctly, and it is suited for those who wish to maintain a high level of health and well-being.

(4)   Yishou (hold attention)
Yishou Dantian, where one concentrates on the point below the navel, is used exclusively in Vitalizing Qigong. It is essential that one dispell all distracting thoughts and focus on Dantian to reach the state of Rujing if good results are desired. Refer back to the previous section for details on Yishou Dantian.

The step-by-step instruction on how to combine all the steps in Vitalizing Qigong will be detailed below for each of the above mentioned methods of breathing. Choose the breathing method which most suits your physical condition and practice it regularly for the best results.

Quiet Breathing Technique

This form of Vitalizing Qigong is suited to people who are old, physically weak, or have respiratory problems.

(1)   Relax mind and body—Relaxation Qigong can be done.

Fig. 36

(2)   Diaoshen (adjust posture)
1.   Sit down with both legs crossed so the soles of your feet face outward and your legs are resting comfortably on your feet.
2.   Draw your hips back slightly and keep your head, neck, and back in a straight line. Relax your shoulders and bring your arms forward for the "contained chest" posture (Fig. 36).
3.   Relax your neck muscles and allow your head to tilt forward just slightly; then close your eyes lightly (Fig. 37).
4.   Relax both arms and place them on your lap in front of your lower abdomen with the palms facing up. Either lightly hold one hand in the other (Fig. 38), or simply place one hand over the other.

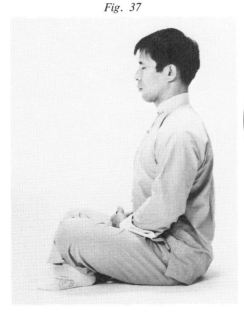

Fig. 37

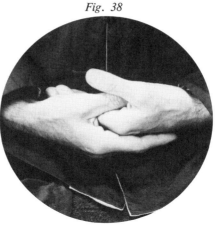

Fig. 38

(3) Diaoxi (regulate breathing)

1. Close your mouth naturally and relax your jaws so that your teeth are just barely touching; then place the tip of your tongue on the roof of your mouth.

2. Inhale through your nose (Fig. 39).

3. Exhale through your nose (Fig. 40).

There is no need to pay any attention to your breathing. Just relax and breathe naturally. The step of Yishou, or concentration on one point, is not necessary with Quiet Breathing. Just keep your body relaxed, hold your spine straight, and continue breathing quietly and rhythmically this way for about half an hour.

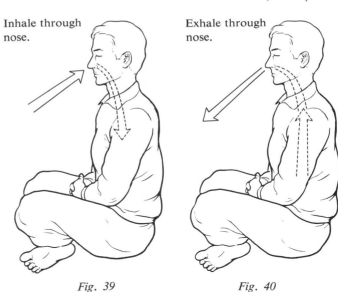

Inhale through nose.

Exhale through nose.

Fig. 39

Fig. 40

Note: Be sure to perform the closing moves described in Relaxation Qigong section after completing this Qigong exercise.

Deep Breathing Technique

The Deep Breathing Technique is suited to those who have problems with neurasthenia or constipation or those who find it hard to keep their concentration.

(1)   Relax mind and body—Relaxation Qigong can be done.

(2)   Diaoshen (adjust posture)—The cross-legged position is used for convenience sake. Refer to Step 2 of Quiet Breathing Technique for a detailed explanation.

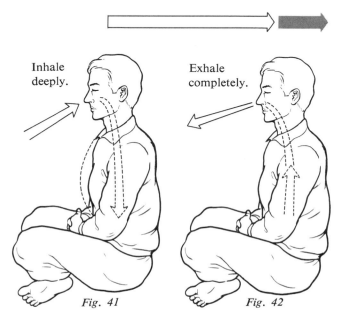

Inhale deeply.

Exhale completely.

Fig. 41   *Fig. 42*

(3)   Diaoxi (regulate breathing)
1.   Close your mouth naturally, relax your jaws so that your upper and lower teeth are just barely touching, and lightly touch the tip of your tongue on the roof of your mouth.
2.   Inhale slowly and gently through your nose for an extended period to draw a deep breath. As you inhale, your chest and abdomen should expand naturally (Fig. 41).
3.   Exhale slowly and gently through your nose for an extended period to exhale completely. As you exhale, your chest and abdomen should go back to normal (Fig. 42).

There is no need for concern even if you are unsuccessful in breathing deeply or if you cannot keep up Deep Breathing for a long time. Work within your own limits and your breathing will become progressively longer and deeper the more you practice.

(4)   Yishou (hold attention)
Keep your attention focused on the Dantian point and do not be distracted by absent thoughts. It may be helpful to imagine a small ball or sphere in your lower abdomen below your navel and to concentrate on this while breathing deeply. Eventually you will reach the calm and serene state of Rujing.

Note: Never practice Deep Breathing right after a meal. Also, be sure to perform the closing moves described in Relaxation Qigong section upon completing this Qigong exercise.

Inverse Breathing Technique

The Inverse Breathing Technique is for basically healthy individuals and is effective for increasing physical energy and maintaining a high level of well-being. Inverse Breathing is widely practiced in China by students of the martial arts.

(1)   Relax mind and body—Relaxation Qigong can be done.

(2)   Diaoshen (prepare posture)—The cross-legged position is used for convenience sake. Refer to Step 2 of Quiet Breathing Technique for a detailed explanation.

(3)   Diaoxi (regulate breathing)

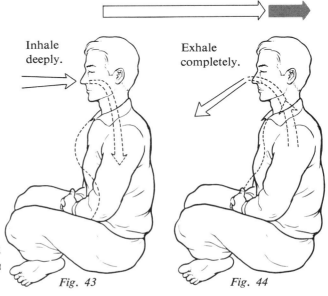

Inhale deeply.

Exhale completely.

Fig. 43   Fig. 44

1.   Close your mouth naturally, relax your jaws so that your upper and lower teeth are just barely touching, and lightly touch the tip of your tongue on the roof of your mouth.

2.   Inhale slowly and gently through your nose for an extended period to inhale completely. As you inhale, expand your chest and suck in your stomach (Fig. 43).

3.   Exhale slowly and gently through your nose for an extended period to exhale completely. As you inhale, allow your chest to return to normal and expand your stomach (Fig. 44).

Be careful not to strain yourself when doing this breathing exercise. Do not be concerned even if the expansion of your chest and stomach is slight in the beginning: The amount of expansion will increase the more you practice. Just concentrate your efforts on breathing deeply and rhythmically in time with the expansion and contraction of your abdominal wall. Give yourself an ample amount of time to master this powerful breathing method.

(4)   Yishou (hold attention)

Keep your attention focused on the Dantian point and do not be distracted by absent thoughts. It may be helpful to imagine a small ball or sphere in your lower abdomen below your navel and to concentrate on this while breathing deeply.

Note: Never practice Inverse Breathing right after a meal. Also, be sure to perform the closing moves described in Relaxation Qigong section after completing this Qigong exercise.

How Much to Practice

Those who are ill should refer to Chapter 5, Qigong for Curing Diseases. Those who just have a generally weak physical constitution or those who are basically healthy and are practicing Qigong for general health, prevention of disease, and longevity should practice once or twice a day. The ideal way to practice is to do thirty minutes to one hour early in the morning and/or before going to bed at night. Beginners should not practice for long periods. It is best to gradually lengthen the practice time as you become more experienced.

Preventive Qigong (Self-administered Massage)
保健功

Preventive Qigong is a series of exercises developed by Dr. Liu Gui-zhen based on traditional Taoist exercises for longevity, which have been practiced in China from ancient times. A large variety of self-administered massage and simple remedial exercises have been handed down in various schools through Chinese history. With a view to popularizing these exercises by taking the useful parts and eliminating the overly complicated parts, in the 1950s, Dr. Liu took the most well-known exercises and organized them into a series of eighteen simple exercises that can be practiced by anyone.

The exercises in Preventive Qigong were all derived from Taoist exercises for longevity, which were traditionally used as preparatory exercises for Zhoutian Gong [周天功], the Circulation of Heaven exercise. In this exercise, Qi or vital energy is circulated around the vertical center of the body (down the front and up the back of the body). Many self-administered massage techniques have been handed down in China as a simple and sure way of generating the Qi, necessary for circulation in the most vital energy channels of the body. Thus, Preventive Qigong is a most basic exercise as an adjunct to other types of Qigong and for cultivating endurance and vitality. Preventive Qigong is an absolute necessity for those who wish to attain a high level of proficiency in Qigong.

Since Inner Regulation Qigong and Vitalizing Qigong both belong to the category of Passive Qigong, where the body is hardly moved at all, Preventive Qigong was formulated to compliment these as a form of Active Qigong, where all parts of the body are massaged and moved. Since Preventive Qigong, in addition to exercising the limbs and all the major joints in the body, includes methods for sharpening the sense organs such as the eyes, nose, and ears, it is a very effective way of maintaining health or otherwise recovering from chronic illnesses. Since these exercises are not in the least strenuous and they are simple to learn, they can be practiced regularly with ease by anyone including elderly persons and those who are weakened by an illness.

It is not necessary to perform every one of the exercises of Preventive Qigong as many times as suggested every time you practice Preventive Qigong. In many cases it is better to reduce the number of repetitions so that all exercises can be completed within half an hour. Since all these exercises can be done in or on a bed, it is best to make a habit of doing the full sequence either in the morning just after getting up or at night just before retiring. When learning these exercises in the beginning, however, it is better to practice just a few of these exercises repeatedly.

Quiet Sitting

Quiet Sitting is almost identical with Vitalizing Qigong practiced in the cross-legged sitting position. This exercise was also formulated by drawing from traditional Buddhist and Taoist meditation practices. The effects of Quiet Sitting are very similar to those of Vitalizing Qigong, but the difference is that Quiet Sitting is a prelude to other Preventive Qigong exercises, whereas sitting and regulating one's breathing is the main part of Vitalizing Qigong. Quiet Sitting is important for relaxing and centering one's Qi in Dantian before beginning Active Qigong.

1. Sit cross-legged in a natural way. Both your calves should cross each other and the soles of your feet should face out. Make yourself comfortable with your legs crossed in this manner and keep your spine straight from your head to your hips. Keep from leaning in any direction. Push your hips back slightly and bring your upper arms a little forward for the "contained chest" posture. Relax your neck muscles and allow your head to tilt forward just slightly. Grasp your thumbs lightly inside your hands and place your fists in your lap and relax your arms. If you find it difficult to relax your arms in this way, you can just place your hands, palms down,

Fig. 45

Fig. 46

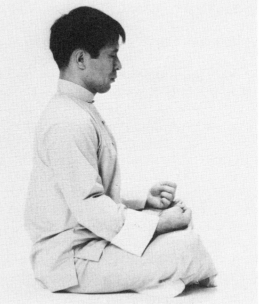

on your thighs. Close your eyes and mouth lightly and place the tip of your tongue lightly on the gums above the back of your upper teeth.

2. Focus your attention on Dantian. This is Yishou Dantian, the most commonly used method for dispelling distracting thoughts. Do not exert yourself in an unnatural way trying to concentrate on Dantian. All you need to do is to keep your attention fixed on this point below your navel. If you are a beginner and find it difficult to concentrate on Dantian, you may skip this step and just relax and breathe in a natural way.

3. Inhale and exhale through your nose fifty times. It is also possible to breathe naturally for several minutes without counting the number of breaths. Practice will allow you to make each breath longer, thinner, and deeper; ideally you will learn deep abdominal breathing in this way. Remember, however, that it requires time to learn to breathe diaphragmatically without any effort, so just keep your breathing natural and even, and do not force yourself to breathe too deeply (Figs. 45 and 46).

Effects: When Quiet Sitting is practiced regularly, you become able to quiet the mind and calm down quickly. Also, since you become able to breathe deeply and relax in short amount of time, this serves as an ideal preparation for performing all the rest of the Preventive Qigong exercises. The more relaxed a person is, the more the circulation of Qi is enhanced.

The effects of this exercise in physiological terms is to enhance the respiratory function of expelling carbon dioxide and absorbing oxygen. Furthermore, circulation is improved throughout the whole body. This exercise is therefore beneficial for respiratory problems such as emphysema and circulatory disorders such as hypertension and heart disease as well as for nervous conditions such as neurosis. It is very helpful in bringing a recovery of physical energy in those who are ill, and it is ideal as a method for preventing disease and maintaining an optimal level of health.

Knocking Teeth

Sit in a natural and comfortable way in the cross-legged position and close your eyes and mouth lightly and focus your attention on Dantian. (You may just continue on from the previous exercise or start with this exercise after finishing some Passive Qigong exercise. This cross-legged position is used in all the exercises of Preventive Qigong except the very last.)

Open and close your jaws in rapid succession so that your teeth make a clicking sound. Do not bring your teeth together too hard. Knock your teeth together in this way for thirty-six times in succession. The traditional practice is to repeat this movement thirty-six times, but there is no need to do this many all the time. Any number of repetitions over ten is generally sufficient. (This also applies to the other exercises in Preventive Qigong. The number of repetitions can be increased or decreased according to the amount of time available.)

Effects: This exercise stimulates circulation in the gums and surrounding tissues to keep the teeth strong, and serves to prevent dental problems. It is especially effective in the cure and prevention of toothaches and gingivitis. Also, this exercise keeps the facial muscles such as the masseter in good tone.

The primary purpose of this exercise, however, is to stimulate the production of the saliva necessary for another Preventive Qigong exercise, Swallowing Saliva.

Tongue Exercise

Keep your mouth closed but open your jaws to stick your tongue between your teeth. Stick your tongue up between your upper teeth and upper lip and begin rotating it down around to the right and make five complete rotations. As you rotate your tongue this way, the top of your tongue should rub over the front of your upper teeth and the bottom of your tongue should rub over the front of your bottom teeth. Repeat this tongue rotation five times in the other direction (Figs. 47–50).

Traditionally the tongue rotation is done eighteen times in each direction, but for beginners this is too tiring for the tongue and some people even find it difficult to rotate their tongue five times in each direction. Therefore, rotating the tongue five times in each direction is enough. Just be careful not to strain your tongue in this exercise.

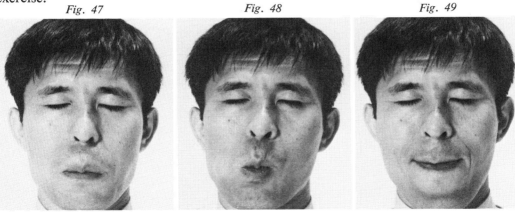

Fig. 47   *Fig. 48*   *Fig. 49*

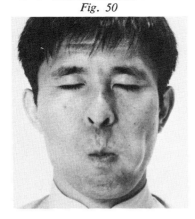

Fig. 50

Effects: This exercise strengthens the tongue and improves the tone of the oris muscles (the muscles around the mouth). This exercise facilitates recovery from facial paralysis when practiced in conjunction with conventional medical treatments or acupuncture. The primary purpose of this exercise along with the last exercise is to facilitate the production of saliva necessary for the next Preventive Qigong exercise.

Swallowing Saliva

1. Keep your mouth closed and rinse the inside of your mouth with the saliva which has been produced by Knocking Teeth and Tongue Exercises. You should cause a swishing sound in your mouth by puckering your lips and alternately filling and emptying your cheeks with air. Do this about thirty-six times in a row. This will cause even more saliva to collect in your mouth.

2. After this, swallow about a third of the saliva in your mouth with a distinct swallowing sound. Imagine that this saliva is being swallowed very deeply to reach all the way down to Dantian. Swallow the remaining two-thirds of the saliva by swallowing in the same manner two more times.

Effects: The Swallowing Saliva exercise can cure and prevent gum diseases. It also stimulates digestive glands to increase the secretion of digestive juices. This serves to improve the appetite and facilitates digestion and the assimilation of nutrients. Imagining that one is swallowing saliva down to Dantian helps to draw the Qi down to Dantian and makes it easier to concentrate on this point and quiet one's mind.

Eye Exercise

1. Open both eyes and rotate them four times counterclockwise and then four times clockwise. Then, keeping your head stationary, alternately look to your left and to your right four times (Figs. 51 and 52). Next, alternately look up and then down four times (Figs. 53 and 54). After this, alternately look to the upper right hand corner and down to the lower left hand corner four times and then to the upper left hand corner and down to the lower right hand corner four times (Figs. 55–58).

These eye movements are traditionally repeated eighteen times, but this many repetitions are not necessary. It is also possible to do this exercise with your eyes

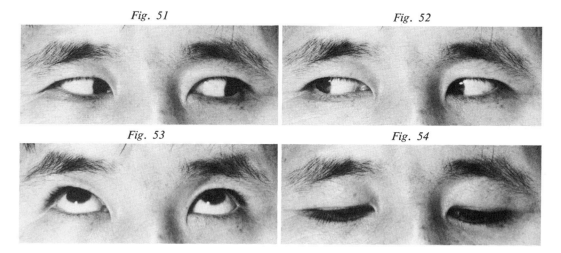

Fig. 51   Fig. 52

Fig. 53   Fig. 54

Fig. 55   Fig. 56

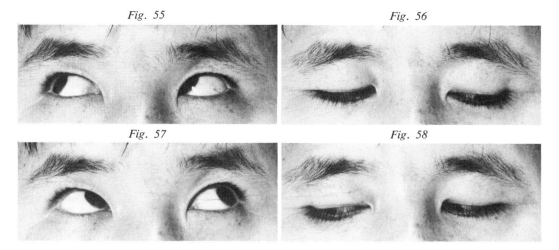

Fig. 57   Fig. 58

closed, but for beginners it is usually hard to do this exercise with the eyes closed. Elderly people should be careful to do the eye movements slowly because it can cause some people to feel dizzy or become nauseous.

2. Rub the inside edges of your thumbs together briskly so they heat up with friction and then close your eyes and rub your eyes lightly with the edge of your thumbs four times, going from the inside to the outside. Next, briefly rub the back

Fig. 59

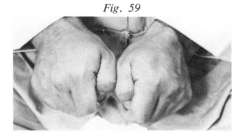

of your thumbs together and rub over your eyebrows from the inside to the outside edge (Figs. 59–61).

3. Rub your thumbs together in the same way as above and massage the important acupuncture points around the eyes (see Appendix).

Fig. 60   Fig. 61

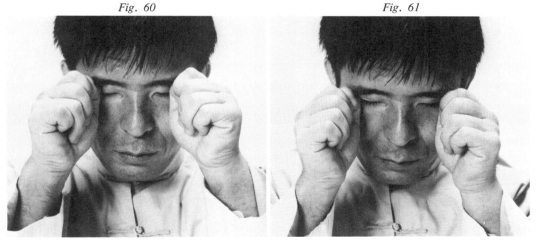

Effects: The eye exercise increases circulation in the eye muscles as well as within the globe of the eye to improve its functioning. This exercise is therefore helpful in curing and preventing eye problems and serves to improve eyesight. Similar eye exercises applying traditional acupuncture points are taught to primary and junior highschool students in China, and this has substantially reduced the incidence of myopia in Chinese school children.

Nose Rub

Rub the back of your thumbs together until they heat up with friction. Next, place them on either side of your nose, covering the acupuncture points next to the nose (see Appendix). Then rub your nose up and down on both sides. Traditionally this is done eighteen times, and although it is not necessary to do this many repetitions every time, it is recommended that you do the full count for simple exercises like this one (Figs. 62 and 63).

Fig. 62 *Fig. 63*

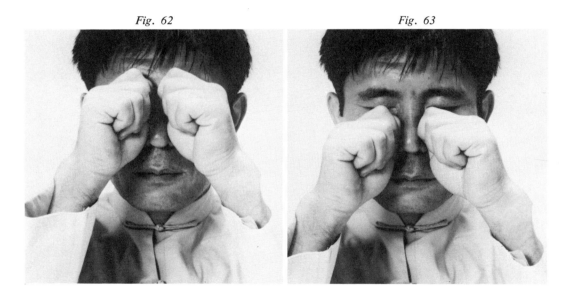

Effects: This exercise serves to strengthen the resistance of the upper respiratory tract, so it has a pronounced effect in preventing rhinitis and colds. Also, it is effective in helping cure allergic rhinitis and other chronic nasal problems. At times this one exercise can be instantly effective in clearing up nasal congestion.

Face and Scalp Rub

1. Rub the palms of you hands together briskly to warm them up (Fig. 64). Then rub your face with both hands from your forehead down to your chin and back up your face so that the center of your palms come over your eyes. When rubbing

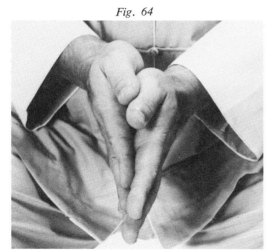

Fig. 64

upward, you may choose to move both hands slightly out to both sides so that the up-and-down movements of your hands draw oblong circles on both sides of your face. Repeat this face rub thirty-six times (Figs. 65–67).

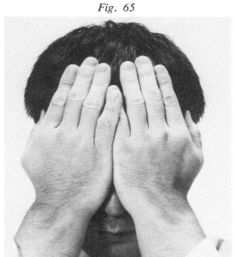

Fig. 65

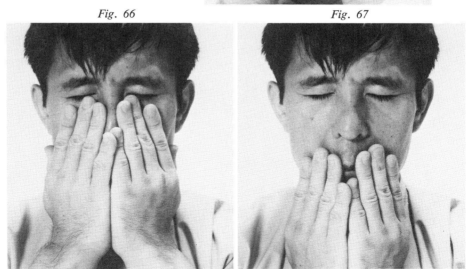

Fig. 66   *Fig. 67*

2. Line up the tips of your fingers of both hands on your front hairline and use your fingers to comb your hair to the back of your head. Your fingertips should rub your scalp as they move toward the back of your head. Start over again at the front hairline and repeat this several times.

Fig. 68

3. After this, place the fingertips of your favored hand on your front hairline and start massaging your scalp toward the back with a grasping and releasing motion to move your hand toward the back of your head as if it were crawling over your scalp. Your hand will reach the back of your head by the alternate grasping and relaxing action. Repeat this scalp massage several times in a row (Fig. 68).

Effects: This exercise improves circulation in the facial muscles and the scalp. Increased facial circulation leads to improved complexion and adds luster to one's facial skin. Since this exercise stimulates the facial nerves, it is also beneficial for cases of facial paralysis.

Ear Exercise

1. Grasp your earlobes between the sides of your bent index fingers and thumbs and pull them down five times (Fig. 69).
2. In the same manner as above, grasp the top of your ears and pull them up five times (Fig. 70).
3. Press the base of your thumbs against the front of your ears to rub them backward and then rub them forward so that your ears fold forward and cover the opening. Rub backward once more so your ears return to their original position.

Fig. 69   *Fig. 70*

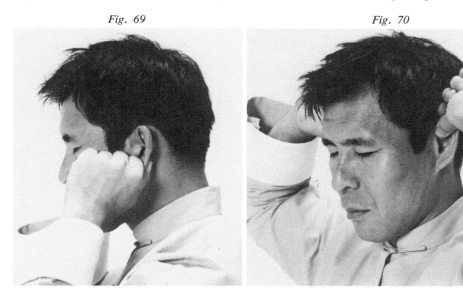

Fig. 71

Fig. 72

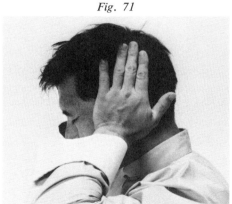

Fig. 73

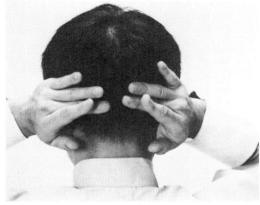

Repeat this several times (Figs. 71 and 72).

4. Next, cover your ears with the palm of your hands and hold the back of your head with the four fingers of both hands. Press your index fingers against the middle fingers and then release them all of a sudden so they snap down on the back of your head (Figs. 73 and 74). The index fingers are snapped in this way over the acupuncture point Fengchi (see Appendix). This snapping should be just light enough to cause a short ring in your ears each time. The traditional Chinese name for this is "drumming the heavens."

Fig. 74

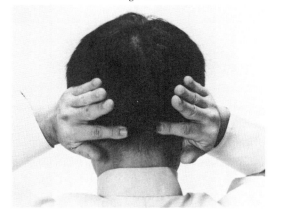

Effects: Massaging the outer ear stimulates the auditory nerve and increases its threshold to thereby improve hearing. This exercise also is useful for the cure and prevention of tinnitus because it provides the cerebrum with mild stimulation which helps to coordinate the function of the central nervous system. Also, it stimulates the circulatory and respiratory centers in the medulla oblongata to some extent and improves the functioning of the heart and lungs. This exercise is also known to be effective for dizziness and headaches.

Neck Exercise

1. Open your eyes (the eyes remain open in all of the exercises that follow). Rest both hands on your thighs and straighten your back (Fig. 75).
2. From the upright position, slowly bend your head down to the left in three successive stages (Fig. 76).
3. Return your head to the upright position and slowly bend your head down to the right in three stages.
4. Return your head to the upright position and this time slowly bend your head forward in three stages (Fig. 77).
5. Return your head to the upright position and slowly bend your head backward in three stages (Fig. 78).
6. After returning your head to the upright position again, slowly rotate your head in big circles three times around to the left (Fig. 79).

Fig. 75　　　　　*Fig. 76*

Fig. 77

Fig. 78

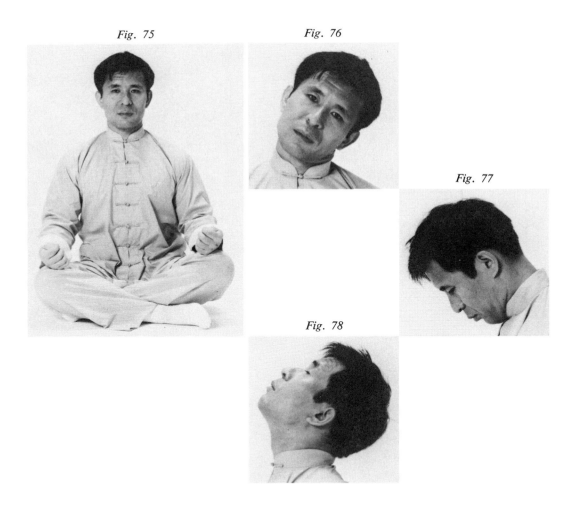

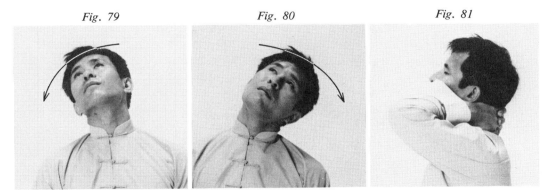

Fig. 79   *Fig. 80*   *Fig. 81*

7. Rotate your head around in the other direction three times in the same manner (Fig. 80).

8. Clasp your hands together by interlocking your fingers and hold the back of your neck. Pull your hands forward as you tilt your head back so that these movements are in opposition to each other. Repeat this movement up to nine times (Fig. 81).

Effects: This exercise is based on the neck movements which many people perform as a matter of habit to release tension from the neck and shoulders. Since it stretches the muscles and tendons of the neck, it is beneficial for cervical problems, and minor neck problems can be cured this way. Also, this exercise improves circulation in the neck and shoulders to reduce tension and pain in the neck and shoulder area and alleviates dizziness.

Shoulder Massage

1. Grasp the tip of your left shoulder in your right hand and massage and rub it in a circular motion counterclockwise for eighteen times and then clockwise for eighteen more times (Figs. 82 and 83).

Fig. 82   *Fig. 83*

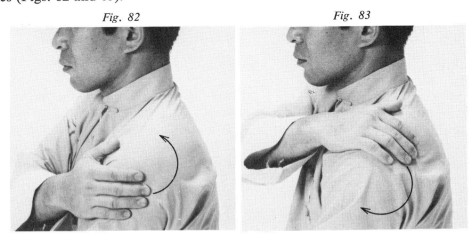

2. Next, grasp the tip of your right shoulder in your left palm and massage it in the same way in both directions.

The number of circles is not so important as long as you briskly rub around the tip of your shoulders and get it warmed up with friction.

Effects: This exercise improves circulation around the shoulder joint and is therefore effective in healing and preventing shoulder problems such as periarthritis. However, when the mobility of the shoulder joint has been greatly impaired, or the problem has existed for a long time, just this exercise alone is not sufficient to effect a cure.

Arm Extension

Fig. 84

1. Make fists with both hands but do not clench them tightly. Just as with the hand placement during Quiet Sitting, it does not matter whether you grasp your thumbs inside your fists or you keep the thumbs on the outside. Bend both of your elbows at a right angle and hold your fists with the palms facing upward (Fig. 84).

Fig. 85

2. Slowly extend your right arm out in front of you and keep the fist facing up. Just before your arm is fully extended, quickly increase the speed of the arm extension to effect a full stretch. As you extend your right arm out, slowly draw your left elbow back so that your left arm goes back with the quick thrust. Turn your upper body fully at the waist as you extend your arm forward so that when both arms are completely stretched out this way, they form a straight line from the extended fist across both shoulders to the cocked elbow. Your body should lean forward slightly with the full extension, and you must look to the back (Fig. 85).

3. Slowly return to the original position and bring both fists back to your side with the palm side up.
4. Slowly extend your left arm out in front of you and draw your right arm back and give a quick thrust at the end to effect a full extension in the same way as above.

Do this exercise alternately on each side so as to twist your upper body back and forth. Repeat this up to eighteen times.

Effects: This exercise increases the flexibility of the spine as well as the shoulder joints and elbow joints. The muscles in the arm and torso are exercised to improve circulation in the upper part of the body. Also, the twisting of the upper body has a massaging action on the internal organs and facilitates their functioning. Since most of the twisting is done at the waist or the lumbar joints, the lumbar area is exercised to effectively prevent low back pain.

Waist Rotation

Fig. 86

1. Place your hands on your knees in the cross-legged seated position (Fig. 86). Another possible variation is to clasp both hands together and place them over your lower abdomen.
2. Slowly begin to rotate your upper body down to the left and around to the front. Begin by relaxing all of the muscles in your upper body as much as possible, especially those in your back and waist area. Keep your upper spine as straight as you can and let your upper body go down to the left and then rotate at your waist to go out to the front and around to the right and then back up to the sitting position. Instead of returning to the fully upright

Fig. 87

Fig. 88

Fig. 89

Fig. 90

Fig. 91

position, however, lean back as much as you can while keeping your spine straight and your hands on your knees. Exhale as you move down and around, and inhale as you come back to the upright position (Figs. 87–91).

3. After rotating once down to the left and around to the right, do the exact opposite and slowly rotate down to the right and around to the left. The breathing is just the same—you exhale as you go forward and inhale as you return to the original position.

The Waist Rotation, alternating in each direction, is repeated sixteen times. (Five repetitions are generally sufficient for a quick routine.)

Effects: Rotating one's waist in this manner stretches the muscles in the waist and pelvic area and works to strengthen these muscles. This exercise is valuable along with the preceding Arm Extension and the subsequent Back Rub for the treatment and prevention of low back pain. There are many vital points in the low back area that are closely related to the kidneys in Oriental medicine. The kidneys in Oriental medicine are the vital organs which store "essence" (the basic substances necessary for building and maintaining our body). In other words, it is considered to hold the "essence of life." Rotating the waist stimulates these kidney points on the back and is thus thought to have an effect of strengthening the kidneys. In addition to kidney points, there are also points associated with the large and small intestines next to the spine on the lower back. Aside from the beneficial effect from the stimulation of these points by rotating at the waist, this exercise also has a massaging action on the internal organs and therefore facilitates the function of the digestive system and improves digestion and assimilation.

Back Rub

Fig. 92

Begin by briskly rubbing the palm of your hands together to heat them up with friction. After this, open your shirt to expose your back and put both hands on your lower back. Then briskly rub your back on either side of your lumbar spine. You can rub your back by either moving both hands up and down together or by moving up with one hand and down with the other; use the method which works the best for you. Repeat the up-and-down motion eighteen times, or as many times as it takes to warm up your lower back (Fig. 92). In cold environments, instead of baring your back, you can rub your back over your shirt.

Effects: As mentioned with the last exercise, Waist Rotation, many points related to the kidneys are located on the lower back, so the Back Rub also stimulates and strengthens the kidneys, which traditionally are the source of vitality. This exercise improves circulation in the lumbar area and relieves fatigue in the back area, so it is effective in the treatment and prevention of chronic back pain. In addition to this, the Back Rub is an important exercise for alleviating the various symptoms associated with dysmenorrhea and menopause.

Sacral Rub

Fig. 93

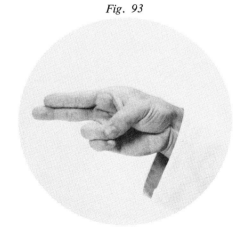

Remain in the same seated position with your back exposed as in the preceding exercise. Extend the index finger and middle finger of both hands and hold the ring fingers and little fingers with your thumbs. Then use your pointed index and middle fingers to briskly rub both sides of your sacrum and coccyx. Just as in the last exercise, you can either move both hands up and down together or rub up with one hand and down with the other (Figs. 93 and 94).

86

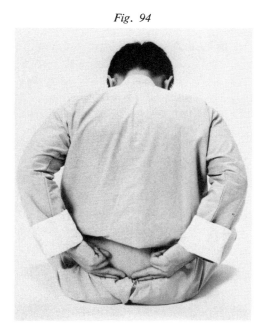

Fig. 94

Effects: The Sacral Rub strengthens the kidneys by the same principle as the Back Rub, so it is also beneficial for low back pain. The acupuncture points massaged by this exercise are the Eight Liao Points of the sacrum (Shangliao [B-31], Ciliao [B-32], Zhongliao [B-33], and Xialiao [B-34] on either side of the sacral crest). These points each correspond to dorsal sacral foramina where the sacral nerves leave the sacrum. The sacral nerves are closely connected with the function of the reproductive organs, so the Sacral Rub is effective in cases of premature ejaculation and impotence for men and dysmenorrhea and menstrual cramps in women. This exercise also stimulates the nerves leading to the anus, and this is beneficial in cases of hemorrhoids and prolapse of the anus.

Dantian Rub

1. Briskly rub your hands together to heat them up with friction. Open the front of your shirt to expose your abdomen and place your left hand over Dantian. You can place your right hand over your left hand or otherwise do this exercise with just one

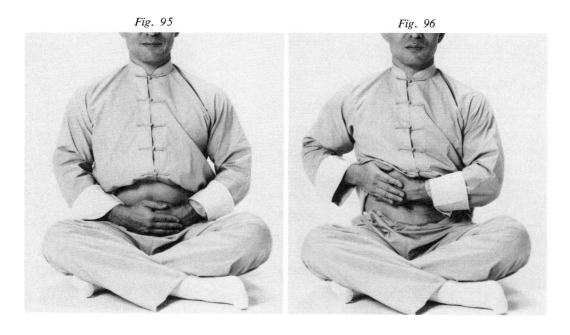

Fig. 95   *Fig. 96*

hand. Rub around your abdomen in a clockwise circular motion. Your hand should follow the course of the large intestine in the order of the ascending colon, the transverse colon, and the descending colon and then return to Dantian. Traditionally, this circular motion was repeated eighty-one times, but ten to twenty times is sufficient for a quick routine (Figs. 95 and 96).

2. Briskly rub your hands together once more and this time place your right hand over Dantian. You can place your left hand over your right hand or work with just one hand. This time rub just around your navel in a counterclockwise direction for the same number of times.

Effects: The Dantian Rub has the same effects as the two preceding exercises, Back Rub and Sacral Rub, in that it strengthens the kidneys. Many vital acupuncture points associated with the internal organs are located on the abdomen and this massage stimulates these points to strengthen not only the kidneys but all the visceral organs. Also since the abdomen is massaged and circulation is improved in the visceral organs, their functional condition is improved. Digestion and assimilation are thereby facilitated, and in addition, tension in the abdomen as well as constipation can be relieved.

Also, just as in the preceding exercise, the Dantian Rub is effective for male sexual problems such as premature ejaculation and impotence. The best way to obtain this benefit is for a man to cup his testicles in one hand and do the Dantian Rub with his other hand. In this practice it is recommended that eighty-one rotations around the abdomen be performed with each hand. This practice serves to increase stamina and strengthen the kidneys, which are traditionally related to the reproductive function in the Orient.

Fig. 97

Knee Massage

Place both hands over your knees in the cross-legged seated position and rub and massage around your kneecaps for up to one hundred times until your knees become warm. You may instead choose to just massage around your knees for several minutes instead (Fig. 97).

Effects: The Knee Massage improves circulation in the knees and strengthens the legs, so it is useful for the treatment and prevention of knee problems which result from overwork or from aging.

Yongquan Massage

1. From the cross-legged position, either straighten your right leg a little or place your right foot on your left leg so that you can reach the sole. Hold your right ankle with your right hand and extend the index and middle fingers of the left hand to rub the Yongquan point with these fingers moving back and forth in line with the foot. Traditionally this rubbing motion was repeated eighty-one times, and there are people in China who do just this exercise thirty minutes everyday. However, you do not need to do this massage any longer than it takes to warm up the back of your foot (Fig. 98).

2. After massaging Yongquan on the right foot, place your left foot over your right leg and massage Yongquan on the right with the index and middle fingers of your right hand.

An alternative method of Yongquan Massage is to raise both knees from the cross-legged seated position and to rub Yongquan on both sides at once with both hands (Fig. 99).

Fig. 98

Note: When doing this exercise before retiring, it is best to wash your feet first.

Fig. 99

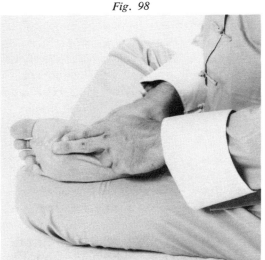

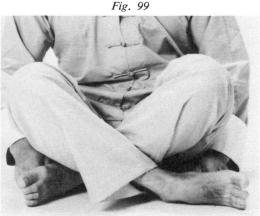

Effects: This exercise regulates the heart function and lowers the blood pressure, so it is good for those with hypertension. It also works to clear one's head, so it is ideal for those with spells of dizziness and those with neurasthenia.

Leg Stretch

1. Sit with both feet stretched straight out in front of you and point your toes up. Interlace your hands together in front of your lower abdomen and slowly bend forward as you exhale. Reach toward your toes with your palms facing forward (Figs. 100–102).

Fig. 100

Fig. 101

Fig. 102

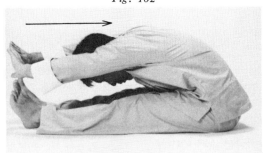

Fig. 103

Fig. 104

2. After you stretch as far as you can go, turn your hands around so the palms face inward and inhale as you slowly return to the original position (Figs. 103 and 104). As you come back up, imagine that you are drawing fresh Qi into your Dantian with your hands. Bend forward and come back up thirty times in this manner. Ten times is sufficient if your time is limited.

Effects: The Leg Stretch increases metabolism and facilitates physiological functions all through the body, but it is particularly effective for back problems. The muscles and tendons of the pelvis, thighs, and legs are extended and this strongly effects the lumbar area. This exercise is effective for relieving muscular fatigue and preventing back pain. However, caution is advised in cases of acute low back pain.

Stepping Qigong 行步功

Stepping Qigong (Xinbu gong) is another type of Active Qigong which is widely practiced among the Chinese. The main feature of these exercises is that movements of the whole body including steps are combined with breath control and the repetition of a special phrase (repeating a phrase, however, is optional). The emphasis is on slow and coordinated movements in synchronization with one's breathing. A point is made of concentrating on Dantian from the beginning stance, and this center or focal point is maintained throughout the entire sequence of exercises. It is very important that your energy be kept centered on Dantian while making a movement with your arms or shifting your weight from one foot to another. You must visualize your energy as extending out from Dantian, which is below your navel, to the limb that is moving. This will allow you to keep your movements steady and flowing and will also enable you to stay in balance.

Practice each exercise for at least ten minutes when you are first learning Stepping Qigong exercises. The total amount of time for practicing the complete sequence should be around thirty minutes. These exercises can be practiced up to four times a day. The entire sequence of exercises in Stepping Qigong can be practiced in order, or otherwise you can practice just a few of the exercises as desired after completing the Basic Stance to suit your physical condition and circumstances.

Basic Stance

Every time Stepping Qigong is practiced one should begin and finish with the Basic Stance. It is very important to begin these exercises in a physically relaxed and mentally composed state. Also, holding this stance for a few minutes after finishing Stepping Qigong is essential for storing Qi and enhancing health.
1.   Calm your mind, still your breath, and relax your body.
2.   Stand straight with your feet about shoulder-width apart and keep your knees just slightly bent. Let your arms hang loosely by your side with your palms facing in. Keep your chest slightly to the inside (contained chest). Hold your head upright and draw your chin in just a little. Keep your spine straight by imagining a plumb line going from the top of your head down through your spine.

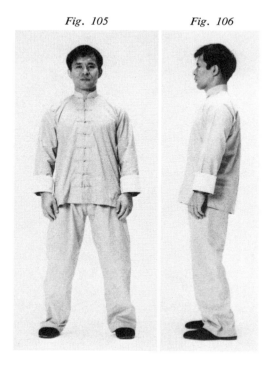

Fig. 105   *Fig. 106*

3. Close your eyes but leave them open just enough to admit a thin streak of light and look straight ahead. Relax and pay attention to your breathing and let go of all distracting thoughts.

4. After your breathing becomes slowed down and your mind is completely calm, shift your gaze to the tip of your nose or close your eyes completely and visualize your Dantian (Yishou Dantian). Imagine your Dantian and keep your attention fixed on this point below the navel. Be sure not to tense your lower abdomen in an effort to concentrate on Dantian.

5. Keep your mouth lightly closed and your teeth loosely together and touch the tip of your tongue gently on the roof of your mouth. You must not close your mouth tightly or bite down; your mouth and jaws must remain totally relaxed. Continue to breathe calmly and naturally this way for a few minutes. It is also possible to count up to fifty breaths in this stance (Figs. 105 and 106).

Effects: The Basic Stance has the same purpose in Stepping Qigong as Quiet Sitting does in Preventive Qigong. In other words, the Basic Stance serves to relax and calm down those who have just set aside work or daily activities to practice Qigong. In addition to getting a person mentally and physically in tune with the calm and slow pace of these exercises, breathing deeply in a relaxed state enhances the function of the lungs and facilitates circulation to increase gas exchange and the supply of nutrients to all parts of the body. In this way the Basic Stance also serves to relieve fatigue.

Drawing in Qi

Drawing in Qi can be done in two ways; either (A) both arms can be rotated inward in a big circle or (B) they can be rotated outward in a big circle. These two methods are explained below.

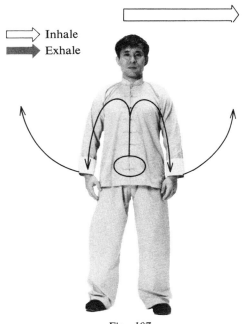

⇨ Inhale
⇨ Exhale

Method (A)

1. After you have become totally relaxed and calm in the Basic Stance, visualize the Qi or vital energy in your Dantian, which you have been concentrating on, and imagine that this energy is expanding up your abdomen and out to your arms and down to your hands (Fig. 107).

2. As you inhale slowly, lift your arms out to both sides and raise them over your head. Continue moving your arms around until your wrists cross each other over your head (it does not matter which

Fig. 107

Fig. 108

hand comes in front). As you raise your hands up, imagine that energy from Dantian is causing your hands to rise up to your sides. Also, visualize Qi being drawn into your body through your outstretched hands to fill you up with vital energy from the atmosphere (Figs. 108 and 109).

3.   Keep rotating your arms down in the same direction as you exhale, so that your wrists cross again in front of your lower abdomen and come down to your side. Your palms should face downward naturally as your arms come down. Imagine here that you are storing the Qi collected by the arm movement in your Dantian (Figs. 110–112).

4.   Continue this arm rotation inward in the same way by raising your arms out to your sides again as you inhale. Repeat this arm rotation slowly up to twenty times.

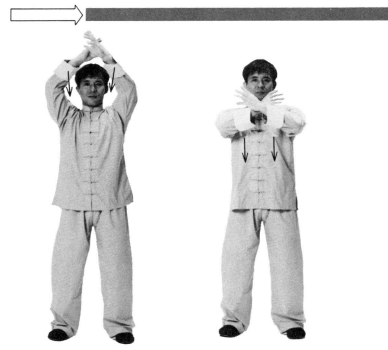

Fig. 109   Fig. 110   Fig. 111

Fig. 112

Fig. 113

Fig. 114

Method (B)

1. Visualize energy rising from Dantian out to your hands as you inhale and slowly raise your arms inward. Cross your arms in front of your lower abdomen and keep raising them so they each go up past the other shoulder (Figs. 113–115)

2. Keep moving your arms up and around so they cross each other over your head and continue to rotate them out down to your sides as you exhale. Turn your palms out naturally to face forward at the top of the circle and down as they descend. Imagine your hands are

Fig. 115

Fig. 116

Fig. 117

drawing in Qi as they circle above your head (Figs. 116 and 117).

3. As your arms travel down to both sides in a big circle, imagine that your hands are storing Qi in your Dantian (Fig. 118).

4. Continue this arm rotation in the same way by raising your arms inward to cross in front of your abdomen again as you inhale. Repeat this arm rotation slowly up to twenty times.

Effects: In this exercise, the arms are rotated in big circles and the chest is expanded fully. As a result of this, respiration becomes deeper. Also, the shoulder joint and all the muscles in the thoracic area are exercised. This keeps tension from accumulating in the neck and shoulders and prevents the occurrence of shoulder problems.

Fig. 118

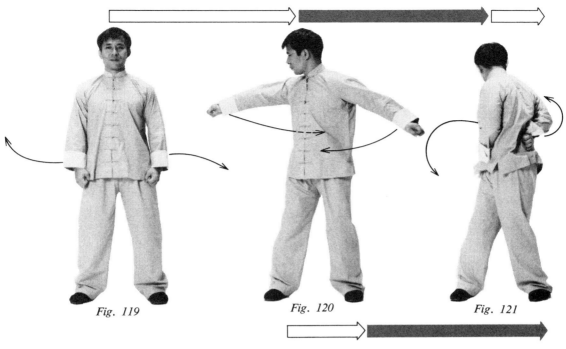

Fig. 119

Fig. 120

Fig. 121

Striking Dantian

1. Make fists loosely with both hands so that they are hollow in the center (Fig. 119).

2. Twist at your waist to turn to your right and strike your Dantian with the palm side of your left fist. Simultaneously strike the Mingmen point (on the same level as Dantian on the lumbar spine) with the back of your right fist (Figs. 120 and 121). Then quickly turn in the opposite direction and strike the same points with the opposite hands (Figs. 122 and 123). Keep turning back and forth and allow your arms to swing around loosely. Lightly strike Dantian and Mingmen repeatedly by the momentum of your turning movements.

Fig. 122

Fig. 123

Synchronize your breathing and your turning movements so that the number of strikes you make with your fists corresponds to the number of breaths you take. Repeat this exercise up to twenty times in each direction.

Once you become used to this exercise, you can perform it while stepping forward with each turn you make (Figs. 124–128). The exercise of striking Dantian while

96

walking can be practiced for up to ten minutes. Repeated practice of this exercise will improve your physical condition by increasing the range of movement in your lumbar vertebrae and by strengthening your spine and pelvic muscles. In turn this will increase the amount you are able to turn at your waist and the extent of your arm rotations.

Effects: This is one of the traditional remedial exercises of China that is regarded as being specially beneficial because of the compounded effect of the light pounding on the back and stomach with the exercise of turning the waist. Striking Dantian below the navel and Mingmen on the lumbar spine shakes the organs inside the abdominal cavity and improves circulation in these organs. Also, just as in Arm Extension and Waist Rotation of Preventive Qigong, the turning at the waist massages the internal organs and improves their function. Both shaking and massaging of the internal organs have a powerful combined effect on the function of these organs. This improves digestion and assimilation and increases the appetite to strengthen one's constitution. In addition twisting at the waist is good for the treatment and prevention of chronic low back pain.

Fig. 124   *Fig. 125*

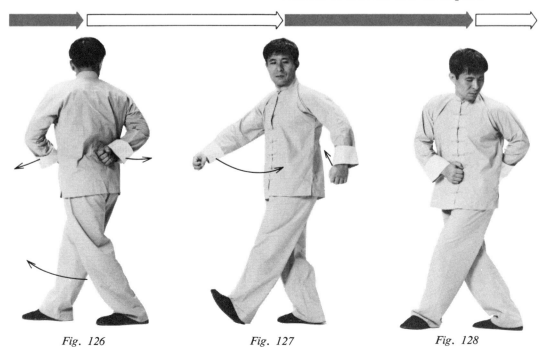

Fig. 126   *Fig. 127*   *Fig. 128*

Watching Hands

Watching Hands is very similar to Cloud Hands, which is part of the Eight Basic Tai-Chi Forms introduced in Chapter 4. The Watching Hands exercise of Stepping Qigong, however, can be performed either in a stationary position or while taking steps to the side. These two methods are each explained below.

Fig. 129 *Fig. 130* *Fig. 131*

Stationary Method
1. Stand with your feet spread apart a little wider than shoulder-width. Visualize Qi flowing up from your Dantian and down to your left hand (Fig. 129).
2. Keep your ankles, knees, and hip joints relaxed and shift your weight over to your right leg. Raise your left arm up across to your right side and keep raising it past your right shoulder. Keep your gaze fixed on the palm of your left hand. Imagine that you are looking into a mirror held in this hand (Figs. 130 and 131).
3. Begin to turn to your left and shift your weight back over to your left foot. Keep moving your left hand around in a circle past your face and out to the left side. At the same time, visualize Qi going down to your right hand and raise it inward across your left side up past your left shoulder with the palm facing up (Figs. 132 and 133).
4. Begin to turn to your right and shift your weight back to your right foot. Keep moving your left hand down in a circle out to your left side and move your right hand up and across in front of your face. Shift your gaze to your right hand as it comes up past your face (Figs. 134 and 135).
5. Keep moving your right hand around in a circle down to the right side. The palm of the right hand turns to face out before it travels downward. At the same

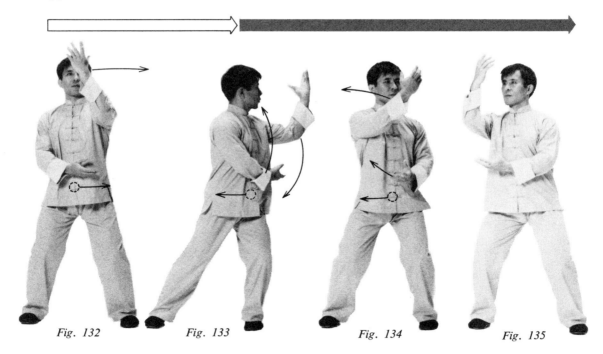

Fig. 132   Fig. 133   Fig. 134   Fig. 135

time, the left hand draws an arc in front of the lower abdomen and comes up on the right side to just in front of the right shoulder. The left hand faces upward naturally as it comes up in a circle (Figs. 136 and 137).

6. Keep moving your right hand down in a circle to your left side and move your left hand up across the front of your face. Shift your gaze to your left hand as it comes up past your face (Fig. 138).

Continue the circling movements of both arms in this fashion as you shift your weight back and forth. Inhale as one hand goes down and the other sweeps in front of your face; exhale as the hand comes up and the other is turned to face out and travel downward. This exercise should be repeated up to thirty times on each side.

Fig. 136   Fig. 137   Fig. 138

Stepping Method

Once you have gained confidence with the stationary method of Watching Hands, you may combine stepping movements. This is not so difficult once you get used to it because the steps are taken in rhythm with the arm movements. The way to step to the left will be explained by referring back to the explanation for the stationary method.

Moves 1 and 2 are the same as in the stationary method.

3. When you move your left hand out to your left side, transfer all your weight over to your left foot and bring your right foot in next to the left (Fig. 139).

4. As you move your left hand down in a circle, shift your weight onto your right foot (Fig. 140).

Fig. 139

Fig. 140   *Fig. 141*   *Fig. 142*

5. Raise your right hand up past your face and move your left hand around in an arc next to your shoulder. As you do this, take a step to the left a little wider than shoulder-width and shift your weight over on to your left foot (Fig. 141).

6. As your left hand comes across your face and moves out to the left again, pick up your right foot and bring it in next to your left foot (Fig. 142).

Continue stepping to the left about twenty times with the Watching Hands exercise, and then switch and begin to step to the right in the opposite way. This is done by bringing the left foot next to the right as the right hand moves out to the right and stepping to the right as the left hand moves out to the left.

Effects: The arm rotation and the turning of the waist in this exercise improves the mobility of the shoulder, elbow, and wrist joints as well as the intervertebral joints. The lower half of the body is also exercised by the turning and stepping movements. In other words, circulation is improved throughout the whole body and this strengthens one's constitution.

Primary Stepping

Primary Stepping is one of the most difficult exercises to master in Stepping Qigong, but it is the most fundamental. In this exercise, you must move forward in balance while also keeping your eyes on the movements of the hands. You must practice until breathing is synchronized with movement so that your attention, breathing, and physical movements are in harmony.

1.   Assume the Basic Stance and relax as you concentrate on Dantian (Fig. 143).
2.   Bend your knees a little more and slowly shift your weight over to your right foot as you inhale. At the same time, imagine Qi flowing from Dantian down into your right foot. As you do this, gently form fists with both hands at your sides (Fig. 144).
3.   Continue to inhale as you shift completely over onto your right leg. Lift your left foot and bring it next to the right foot with the heel lifted slightly and the toes lightly touching the ground. As you do this, keep raising your fists up past waist level with your elbows comfortably bent (Fig. 145).

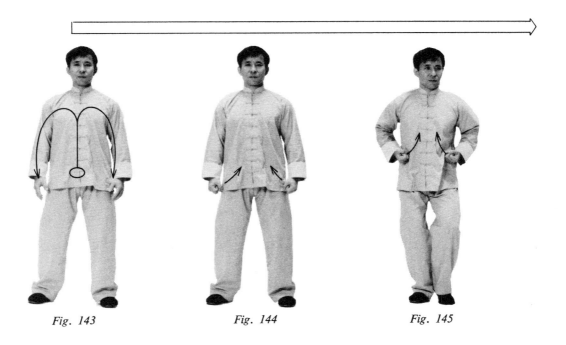

Fig. 143   Fig. 144   Fig. 145

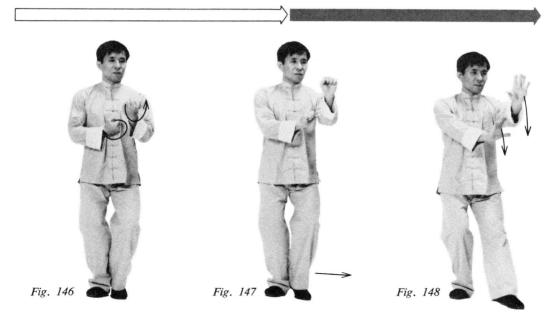

Fig. 146   Fig. 147   Fig. 148

4. Exhale as you take a step forward diagonally to the left, toes first, onto the left foot. Continue raising your arms and open your hands along with the step and push out quickly to the left at a diagonal so both hands face out. Your left hand comes to chest level and your right hand comes a little higher than the navel. Keep your shoulders and arms relaxed and do not straighten your elbows completely. Imagine that you are discharging Qi from the palm of your hands as you push forward rapidly (Figs. 146–148).

5. Continue to exhale as you move forward onto your left foot. Slowly shift your weight forward onto your left foot after the heel contacts the ground. As you move forward, push your hands down together in front of Dantian. (Your hands should form a semicircle with your thumbs and index fingers.) Keep your shoulders relaxed and your elbows comfortably bent. It is important that your shoulders and arms be relaxed as you press down (Fig. 149).

6. Begin to inhale as you bend into your left knee and move forward onto your left foot. Imagine Qi flowing from Dantian down into your left foot. Gently form fists once again as you raise your hands (Fig. 150).

Fig. 149   Fig. 150

Fig. 151   Fig. 152   Fig. 153

7. Continue to inhale as you shift completely over onto your left leg and lift your right foot to bring it next to the left foot with the heel lifted slightly and the toes lightly touching the ground. As you do this, keep raising your fists up past waist level with your elbows comfortably bent (Fig. 151).

8. Exhale as you step forward diagonally to the right, toes first, onto your right foot. As soon as you touch down, push forward diagonally to the right by opening the fists so they face out. Your right hand comes to chest level and your left hand comes a little higher than the navel (Fig. 152).

9. Continue to exhale as you move forward onto your right foot. Slowly shift your weight forward onto your right foot after the heel contacts the ground. As you move forward, push your hands down together in front of Dantian. (Your hands should form a semicircle with your thumbs and index fingers.) Keep your shoulders relaxed and your elbows comfortably bent. It is important that your shoulders and arms be relaxed as you press down (Fig. 153).

This sequence of stepping forward and pushing out and then down in unison with the outgoing breath is repeated to move forward in a zigzag fashion. If there is not much room, you can change the direction of each step slightly to move in a circle. Practice Primary Stepping for about five minutes when performing it in sequence with other exercises of Stepping Qigong. Otherwise it may be practiced by itself for up to half an hour. Do this exercise slowly in the beginning so as to get all the movements coordinated with your breathing. It is possible to practice the stepping movements and the arm movements separately and later put the two together in time with your breathing. Just be sure to step forward slowly and smoothly in a balanced and coordinated fashion.

Effects: In this exercise, the movements of the arms and legs must be perfectly coordinated with your breathing along with the shifting of weight with each step. Further, to keep your mind from wandering, your eyes must be kept on the hands as they move forward and down. Thus, the three elements of awareness, breathing, and movement of the limbs are integrated with the movement of your center of gravity forward to produce a smooth and steady motion. Once you learn to harmonize the mind and body this way, it becomes possible to experience the centering of energy in Dantian. This is a vital step which is essential for the effective practice of all Qigong exercises. For this reason, Primary Stepping is a fundamental exercise which is a key to experiencing and appreciating the benefits of Qigong.

Balance Stepping

Like most other exercises of Stepping Qigong, Balance Stepping can be done in place or by taking steps. Initially practice this exercise without taking steps. The movements are basically the same whether you step forward or not. After you learn how to coordinate the breathing with the movements, you can begin to take steps forward.

Stationary Method
1. Stand straight with your feet together and concentrate on Dantian. As you inhale, raise your arms out to your side up past shoulder level. At the same time raise your left leg while bending it at the knee so the thigh is parallel with the ground. Keep your left foot as relaxed as possible and let the toes point down (Figs. 154 and 155).
2. Pause momentarily with your arms and leg raised in the above position. Then as you exhale, slowly lower your arms back down and put your left foot back down where it was (Fig. 156).
3. As you inhale, once more raise your arms out to the side and this time lift your right leg up (Fig. 157).

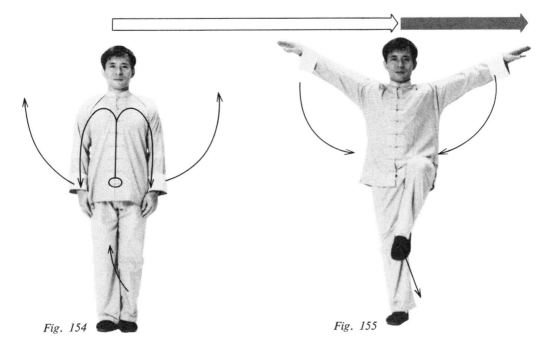

Fig. 154   *Fig. 155*

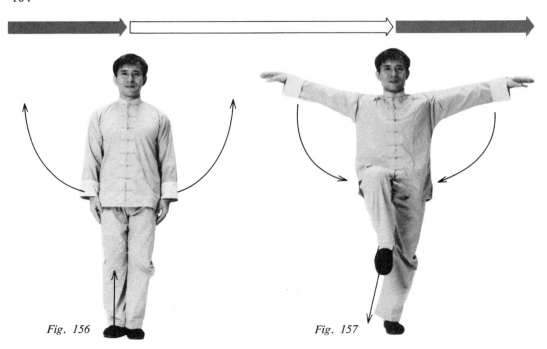

Fig. 156   Fig. 157

4. After a brief pause in the above position, exhale and slowly move your arms and right leg down into the original position.

Stepping Method
1. The starting position and the first move of raising the arms and the left leg are the same as in the stationary method (Figs. 158 and 159).
2. After a brief pause with the arms and left leg raised, lower your arms and leg back down as you exhale. Take a small step as you put your left foot back down (Fig. 160).

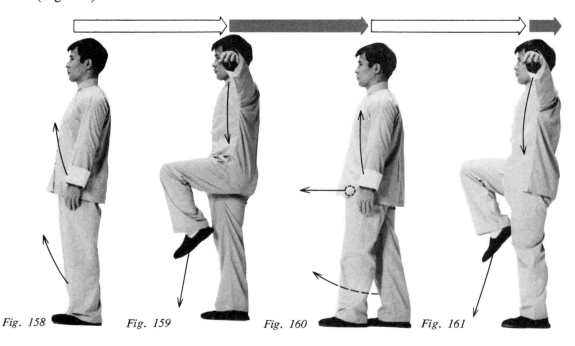

Fig. 158   Fig. 159   Fig. 160   Fig. 161

3. As you inhale, shift your weight forward onto your left leg. Then raise your arms and this time raise your right leg (Fig. 161).

4. After a momentary pause, exhale and slowly move your arms and right leg down, taking a small step forward as you come down (Fig. 162).

Step out slowly and advance cautiously, paying attention to your balance. Remember to keep you focused on Dantian and to extend Qi to your limbs as you raise them. In this exercise also, you can move forward in a straight line or move around in a large circle.

Effects: In this exercise, the body is supported with one leg while the other leg is raised, so this increases circulation to the muscles of the hips and lower limbs and thus improves muscle tone. It is said in the Orient that "aging starts from the legs," and it is common knowledge that the aging process speeds up drastically when a person no longer walks or exercises the legs. Balance Stepping is an important exercise for avoiding the gradual debilitation which accompanies old age and for keeping the limbs strong and supple. This is very useful for preventing diseases like osteoarthritis in the knees. In addition to this, Balance Stepping is good for developing one's sense of balance.

Fig. 162

Kick Stepping

1. Stand straight with your feet together and look straight forward while breathing in a natural and relaxed manner. Keep your attention focused on Dantian (Fig. 163).
2. Take a step forward onto your left foot, and immediately after doing this, swiftly

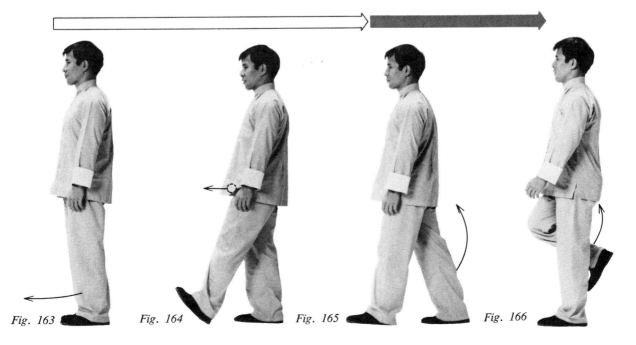

Fig. 163   *Fig. 164*   *Fig. 165*   *Fig. 166*

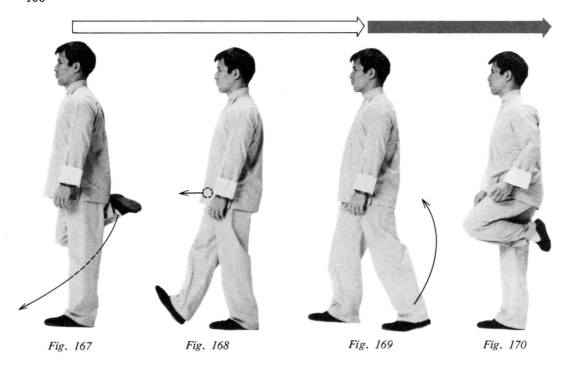

Fig. 167   Fig. 168   Fig. 169   Fig. 170

kick your right foot back up toward your hips by bending the right leg at the knee. (Figs. 164–167).

3. Quickly step forward onto your right leg as it comes down and kick your left leg back up toward your hips in the same way (Figs. 168–170).

4. Do this kick stepping briskly so that your foot reaches up to your buttock. Continue kicking back and stepping forward in this manner.

It usually takes some practice before the heel touches the buttock with each backward kick. Nevertheless, almost everyone eventually becomes able to hit the buttock with the heel so that it makes a slapping sound. To get the most exercise, do this Kick Stepping sequence by taking fifty to one hundred steps in quick succession.

Effects: The whole body is held up with one leg in this exercise as the other foot is kicked back up to the hips. Therefore this exercise also is good for developing a sense of balance. Furthermore this exercise keeps the joints of the leg limber in addition to improving circulation and toning the muscles in the hips and legs.

Rotating Disk

Rotating Disk is also an exercise which can be done in place or by stepping. It is similar to the Watching Hands exercise in that one takes steps to the side in time with arm movements. The stationary method is just the same as the stepping method except that, instead of taking a step, one's weight is shifted back and forth over each foot as the disk is rotated.

Stationary Method

1. Assume the Basic Stance with your feet shoulder-width apart and extend your Qi from Dantian out to your hands (Fig. 171).

2. Inhale and imagine that Qi is filling and lifting your hands. Keep your hands turned down and slowly raise your hands to the level of your navel. Then form the shape of a small circle with your thumbs and index fingers. The two hands forming a circle or "disk" is meant to represent the great symbol of Yin-Yang harmony known as Tai-Chi. After doing this, tilt your head slightly forward to look at your hands. Keep your gaze fixed on your hands all through this exercise (Fig. 172).

3. Keep your shoulders relaxed and

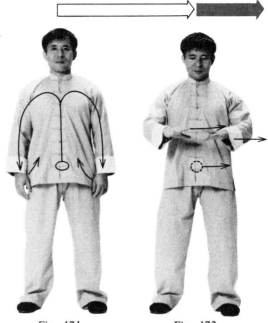

Fig. 171   Fig. 172

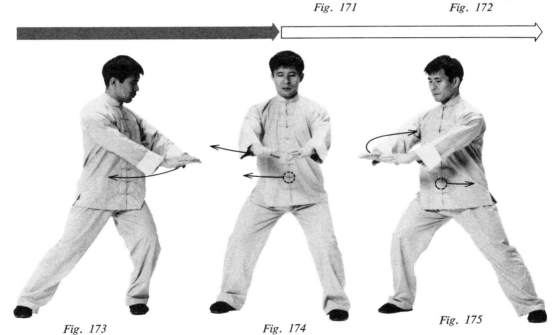

Fig. 173   Fig. 174   Fig. 175

your elbows bent comfortably. Your arms and hands should remain relaxed so that viewed from the top they form a large semicircle with your body. Also, allow your knees to bend a little so that your body sinks down slightly. As you exhale, shift your weight over your left foot and slowly begin to rotate the disk formed by your hands horizontally around to your left. Your waist should turn about forty-five degrees to the left. Slide your right foot out for a wider stance as you move your hands around to your left. Continue to exhale as you rotate the disk around out in front of you (Figs. 173 and 174).

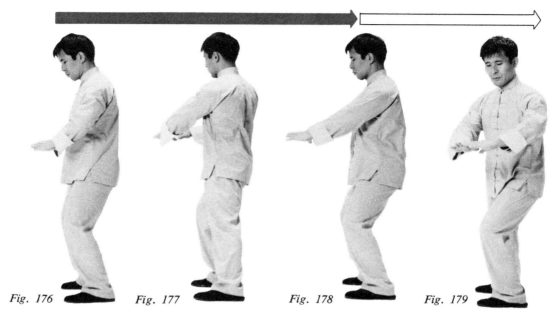

Fig. 176   Fig. 177   Fig. 178   Fig. 179

4. Begin inhaling as you continue rotating the disk around to your right and shift your weight over onto your right foot. Your waist should turn about forty-five degrees to the right (Fig. 175).
5. Continue inhaling and bring the disk back to just in front of your navel. Keep rotating the disk clockwise alternately shifting your weight over each foot as you move the disk around. Reverse the direction after about twenty times and repeat the same number of counterclockwise rotations. Exhale as the disk moves away and inhale as it draws closer. (Figs. 176–179).

Stepping Method
1. The beginning of Rotating Disk, when taking steps, is exactly the same as in the stationary method. From the Basic Stance, inhale as you extend your Qi and raise your hands to form a disk (Figs. 180 and 181).

Fig. 180   Fig. 181

2. As you exhale, slowly begin to rotate the disk on a horizontal plane around to your left. Your waist should turn about forty-five degrees to the left. Shift all your weight over onto your left foot and step out to the right with your right foot. Continue to exhale as you rotate the disk around out in front of you and shift your weight over both feet (Figs. 182 and 183).

3. Begin inhaling as you continue rotating the disk around to your right and shift your weight over onto your right foot. Your waist should turn about forty-five degrees to the right (Fig. 184).

4. All your weight should be over your right foot as you bring the disk back around toward yourself. As the disk approaches your navel, bring your left foot next to your right foot. Complete the inhalation by the time your hands come to the front of your navel (Fig. 185).

Fig. 182   Fig. 183   Fig. 184

Fig. 185   Fig. 186   Fig. 187

5. Keep rotating the disk out to your left as you exhale and shift all your weight over onto your left foot and step out to the right again (Figs. 186 and 187).

6. Keep rotating the disk clockwise and step to your right with each rotation. Rotate the disk for up to twenty times in the same direction. Then reverse and rotate the disk counterclockwise and step to your left in exactly the opposite manner for the same number of times.

The stepping and shifting of weight should be gradual and smooth. When your hands come directly in front of you (both in close and out to the front), your weight must come over both feet equally. All your movements must be gentle but deliberate. Always exhale as you rotate the disk out away from your body and inhale as the disk reaches the farthest point and begins to return. Your lower abdomen should expand with each inhalation and contract with each exhalation. Your breathing must be diaphragmatic so that Qi reaches Dantian with each breath. You will know Qi is reaching Dantian when you come to experience a sense of firmness in your lower abdomen.

Effects: In this exercise it is easier to avoid distracting thoughts and attain a state of mental concentration because one's gaze is kept on the hands all through this exercise as they rotate the disk. This is very useful for achieving the state of Rujing. The movements of stepping to the side and turning the waist exercise the hip, knee, and ankle joints especially to improve circulation, muscle tone, and balance.

Chapter 4

Simplified Tai Chi for Beginners

Qigong and Tai Chi

As explained previously, Tai Chi is important as an adjunct to Qigong therapy. The therapeutic value of Tai Chi should be obvious from the number of diseases it is recommended for in Chapter 5. Tai Chi itself is regarded as one type of Qigong in a broad sense. The similarities between Qigong and Tai Chi which place them in the same general category will be briefly outlined in this chapter.

It was stated in Chapter 1 that all Qigong contains the three common elements of Diaoshen (adjust posture), Diaoxi (regulate breath), and Diaoxin (calm mind). These three principles apply directly to Tai Chi. In respect to Diaoshen, or adjusting posture, Tai Chi has always had very strict rules from its historic beginnings. Tai Chi Quan originated as a type of martial art, and since incorrect posture makes effective defence and attack impossible, proper form was of utmost importance. Some basic rules for posture in Tai Chi include keeping the spine vertical, keeping the head and neck in line with the spine, keeping the chest "contained," and dropping the shoulders and relaxing the arms. It goes without saying that all of these rules are exactly the same as the postural rules for Inner Regulation and Vitalizing Qigong. Another requirement which is essential to all the postural rules of Tai Chi is "total relaxation inside and out." This is one and the same as the relaxation of the mind (inside) and body (outside) stressed repeatedly in Qigong.

In respect to Diaoxi, or breath control, Tai Chi is not as specific as Qigong. Various things are taught about breathing in different styles of Tai Chi, but generally this aspect is given very little attention. Nevertheless, students are usually instructed to inhale through their nose and exhale through either their nose or mouth and to breathe naturally along with their movements. As a student becomes more advanced in Tai Chi, the centering of Qi in Dantian becomes an important requirement, just as in Qigong.

In regard to the principle of Diaoxin, Tai Chi has the maxim "Use your will, not your strength." Thus, in Tai Chi, one's will is exercised to use the absolute minimum of strength. Also, it is necessary that the mind be kept totally quiet and serene and free of all distractions. This is why, just as in Qigong, it is possible to attain the state of Rujing in Tai Chi. This is the reason Tai Chi is sometimes referred to as "moving meditation."

Therefore, the very same principles are emphasized in Tai Chi as in Qigong: that of adjusting posture, regulating breathing, and calming the mind. For this reason Tai Chi is generally regarded as one type of Qigong. While Tai Chi developed independently of the meditative practices of Taoism, which gave rise to Qigong, many aspects of Tai Chi were integrated with Qigong in the course of history. Qigong also influenced Tai Chi in some respects and thus Tai Chi eventually came to be included in the broad category of Qigong exercises.

Eight Basic Tai Chi Forms   八式太極拳

The Tai Chi exercises introduced in this chapter were formulated by Dr. Jiang Haoquan as a simplified version of Tai Chi which takes eight principal exercises from the Yang Style Tai Chi Quan, with a view to providing a quick and simple way to get well rounded exercise. This form of Tai Chi was first introduced in the Anhui Province of China, where it immediately gained popularity, and subsequently it became known throughout China. The Eight Basic Tai Chi Forms have become widely accepted as a simplified version of Tai Chi for beginners.

The Eight Basic Tai Chi Forms cover a complete range of Tai Chi movements by progressing from greater arm movements to greater leg movements, from light to heavy (shifting weight completely over to one leg), from simple to complicated, and from stationary to dynamic. These eight basic forms are designed to instill all the fundamentals of Tai Chi and are arranged in a way that is easy to learn and practice for beginners. The best features of the Eight Basic Tai Chi Forms are that they are easy to learn and remember and that they can be practiced by practically anyone regardless of age. Just this simplified version of Tai Chi, when practiced regularly, is effective in preventing disease, enhancing health, and bringing longevity.

The Eight Basic Tai Chi Forms have two types of forms—stationary and dynamic. In the stationary forms, the same stance is maintained without shifting the weight from one foot to the other, and in dynamic forms weight is shifted and steps are taken. The first and last form of the Eight Basic Forms are stationary forms. All the other forms from Cloud Hands to Heel Kick are dynamic forms. Each of the dynamic forms are a series of arm and leg movements made in one direction followed by the exact same movements in the other direction performed on the opposite side. Thus, you return to the original position after one form is completed by performing the same sequence of moves in both directions. At this point, you can either repeat the same form or go onto the next form after a transition move. Regardless of whether the same form is repeated or not, the movements should flow together smoothly as a slow and continuous motion.

If you are a complete beginner, it is helpful to learn one form at a time and to practice just one form for a set amount of time without counting the number of repetitions. Even those who have never done any Tai Chi before can learn the Eight Basic Tai Chi Forms by carefully studying this chapter and practicing regularly. You should start by studying the figures to piece together the movements and practice the form to get a feel for the general flow of the moves in the form. After this, you should study the explanations for each form for the details and fine points of the moves. Then, you should go on to correct each detail that was not done correctly. It is important to continually strive to refine the moves and perfect the form. You should review the figures and text from time to time to keep from becoming accustomed to doing a form incorrectly. It is perfectly acceptable to practice a form imperfectly, but it is not acceptable to disregard the rules and make no effort to improve on the form each time you practice.

In this book, out of necessity, each of the forms are explained in terms of definite moves or "frames." It should be understood, however, that all the moves must flow together as a continuous and fluid motion, one into the next. After learning each of the eight forms individually, you can connect them together and repeat each form about eight times before going on to the next. This will take from fifteen minutes to half an hour when done slowly. The number of repetitions for each form can be increased or decreased according to the amount of time available.

The first thing that must be done after the proper movements have been mastered is to focus your gaze and attention on the movement of the leading hand. Where the leading hand goes, the eyes must follow. This is an ideal way to keep yourself from getting distracted. The second important thing that must be learned after the movements have been mastered is proper breathing. Generally, you should inhale at the beginning of a move or in "opening" moves, and should exhale during the completion of a move or in "closing" moves. It is very important to coordinate your breathing to match the "opening" and "closing" moves so that you are able to conserve and store vital energy. The third point which must be kept in mind is to make a habit of placing the tongue on the roof of the mouth. When there is excessive salivation, remember to swallow the saliva while visualizing it going down to Dantian. This will help your stomach and improve your digestive function.

1. Beginning Form   太極起勢

Preparation: Stand with your feet shoulder-width apart with the toes pointing straight forward. Hold your head and neck straight and elevate your head slightly, imagining that you are being suspended from a string attached to the very top of your head. Relax your shoulders and let your arms hang loosely by your sides. Relax your chest area so it naturally stays slightly in (remains contained). Breathe naturally and smoothly, and place your tongue on the roof of your mouth (hard palate). Put all distracting thoughts out of your mind and concentrate on Dantian. You should gaze straight ahead into the distance (Fig. 188).

Moves:
1. Raise both hands straight out in front of yourself up to about shoulder level.

(The words front or forward in all explanations which follow indicate this direction.) Your palms should face down with the hands relaxed (Fig. 189).

2. Bend your knees and come down to a half squat. As you do this bring your hands down as if gently pressing downward until they come just above the knees or touch them lightly. Your spine should be kept straight and your eyes should follow the movement of your hands (Figs. 190 and 191).

Inhale

Exhale

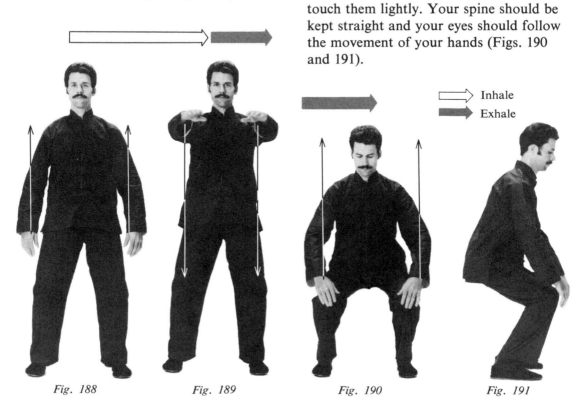

Fig. 188   Fig. 189   Fig. 190   Fig. 191

3. Slowly stand up again, and as you do, raise both arms back up to shoulder level and assume the former position.

Continue doing this form by repeating Moves 2 and 3.

Main points: The arms and hands must remain as relaxed as possible during this form, but the wrists must bend only slightly. The fingertips should raise slightly as the arms travel down, and they should point down slightly as the arms rise. The arms must be lowered gently with the squatting movement so that the palms gently come down to the knees.

It is important to keep the back straight and not to bend the neck forward as you squat down. (Follow the movement of your hands with your eyes, not your head.) Concentrating on Dantian helps keep the back straight and this is the most basic requirement in every form. In all these simplified Tai Chi forms, first learn the basic movements correctly and then integrate the proper breathing and finally, work toward greater concentration and centering on Dantian.

Effects: This is a preparatory form for starting Tai Chi. It serves to activate the muscular and vascular systems and also regulates respiration for the forms which follow. When one is successful in keeping the mind free of distraction to concentrate deeply, this form has a very relaxing and beneficial effect on the central nervous system as well as sense organs including the eyes.

2.   Cloud Hands   雲手

Transition: From the posture of the previous form, with your feet about shoulder-width apart and both hands raised forward, bend your knees slightly and bring both hands down to the level of your navel; keep your back straight (Fig. 192).

Then shift your weight over on to your right foot and slide your left foot over to get in a wide but comfortable stance with both toes pointing forward. Straighten your left leg and bend into your right knee so that most of your weight comes over your right foot. As you do this, turn to your right from the waist while keeping your toes pointing forward as much as possible.

Along with taking a step to the left and shifting over to the right, move your right hand in an arc out to the right so the arm is extended at shoulder level with the palm facing out. At the same time, move your left hand in a smaller arc to just in front of your right shoulder with the palm facing up as if gently holding something. Your gaze should be on the index finger of the right hand as it moves out to the right (Fig. 193).

Fig. 192   *Fig. 193*

Fig. 194   Fig. 195   Fig. 196

Moves:

1. Shift your weight over to your left foot and turn toward your left with your waist as you sweep your left hand past the front of your face. Thus, your left hand goes out to the left at eye level with the palm facing you. At the same time, bring your right arm down in front of your lower abdomen so the palm faces upward. The movement of the arms around to the left should be coordinated with the turning of your waist. Straighten your right leg and bend into your left knee so that most of your weight comes over your left foot. Keep both feet pointing forward as much as possible. Your gaze should be shifted to the left index finger as you begin turning to the left (Fig. 194).

2. Turn your waist to face the left side. Continue moving your left hand out to the left by turning it to face out and gently pushing to the left. At the same time, keep your right hand moving up past your abdomen to just in front of your left shoulder with the palm facing up as if gently holding something. The fingers of the left hand should be about eye level and your gaze should be on the left index finger (Fig. 195).

3. Begin shifting your weight back to your right foot by straightening your left leg and bending into your right knee. Slowly turn your waist back to the right, and as you do, sweep your right hand across the front of your face to the right with the

Fig. 197

palm facing you at eye level. At the same time, bring your left hand down in an arc in front of your lower abdomen on the right side so the palm faces upward. Shift your gaze to the right index finger as you sweep your hand across the front of your face (Fig. 196).

4. Turn your waist to face the right side. Continue moving your right hand out to the right so the arm is extended at shoulder level with the palm facing out. At the same time, keep moving your left hand up from the lower abdomen in a small arc to just in front of the right shoulder with the palm facing up. Your gaze should be kept on the index finger of the right hand as it moves out to the right (Fig. 197).

Continue doing this form on each side by repeating Moves 1 through 4.

Main points: The turning of the body in Cloud Hands should be lead by the hips and waist, not the shoulders. Also, the hip and pelvic joints must be kept relaxed so as to keep the spine upright at all times. Further, both arms must be kept as relaxed as possible with the elbows always slightly bent, even when an arm is extended, so that movements of the arms form circles. The movements of both arms must be coordiatned with the turning of the waist and the bending and straightening of the knees. It is important that most of your weight be shifted over to one foot by bending into the knee and relaxing the other leg that is straightened. If you wish to increase the amount of exercise, the knee can be bent more to shift your weight completely over to one side, and also the span of arm movement can be increased. In addition to this, you can turn further in each direction. However, try to keep the toes of both feet pointing straight forward as much as possible.

Effects: This form mainly consists of shifting weight from one foot to the other and sweeping the arms back and forth. Therefore the amount of exercise is moderate. Nevertheless, when the movements and breathing are correctly synchronized, the functional conditions of the cardiovascular and respiratory systems are improved. Practicing this one form slowly for up to half an hour is beneficial in cases of hypertension and gastric ulcers as well as for arthritis in the hip and knee joints.

3. Brush Knee and Push   搂膝推掌

Transition: Continue from Move 4 of Cloud Hands with your weight mostly over your right foot, your right arm extended at shoulder level, and your left hand in front of your right shoulder (Fig. 198). Turn to the left as you shift all your weight over on to the right foot. Pivot a little on your right heel, if necessary, to point your right

Fig. 198　　　　　　　　*Fig. 199*　　　　　　　*Fig. 200*

foot straight forward. As you turn your waist to the left, reverse the course of your left hand and move it in a circle down past the lower abdomen and up past the left shoulder to the front of the chest on the right side. Also, move your right hand down in a sweeping arc to the front of your lower abdomen on the right side. The right hand faces up and the left hand faces down in opposition to each other as if holding a large ball. Once all your weight is shifted over to the right foot, bend your left leg and draw the left foot in toward the right with just the toes lightly in contact with the ground (Fig. 199).

Moves:

1. Keep both knees bent with all your weight on the right leg. Turn slightly back to face the right side. Raise your right arm by backtracking on the previous movement, to move your hand out to the right at face level with the palm facing in. At the same time, press your left hand down in front of your lower abdomen. Your gaze should be on your right index finger (Fig. 200).

2. Begin turning your waist to the left again and take a big step to the left with your left foot landing heel first. The stance should be wide so that you are balanced and stable. Continue turning your waist to the left as you bend into your left knee and shift about two-thirds of your weight over to your left foot. Your right leg should be extended, but the foot must remain flat on the ground. As you turn to the left, take a step, and shift your weight to the left, push your right hand past the side of your head. The right arm is thus extended at shoulder level with the palm facing out. The left hand, at the same time, travels in an arc to brush just over the left knee from the inside; it ends up with the palm facing down just to the outside of the knee.

Fig. 201   Fig. 202   Fig. 203

Your upper body must be kept vertical through these movements, and also your gaze should be on the right index finger (Figs. 201 and 202).

3. Shift your weight back onto your right foot by bending your right knee and straigtening your left leg. (Keep facing the same direction.) Bring your right hand back to its former position at the side of your head as you shift your weight back, but leave your left hand in the same place at your side (Fig. 203).

4. Turn to the right and pivot your left foot on the heel to make it point forward. Take a step in place onto your left foot and move your hands into position to "hold the ball" on the left side of your abdomen. This time your left hand goes to the bottom and your right hand goes to the top. Shift all your weight over to your left foot and draw the right foot in toward the left (Fig. 204).

5. Turn slightly back to face the left side and bring your left hand back up to your left side to face level. Press down

Fig. 204

Fig. 205

Fig. 206

Fig. 207

Fig. 208

to your lower abdomen with your right hand (Fig. 205).

6. Turn back to the right and take a big step with the right foot, heel first. Meanwhile push in the same direction with your left hand and brush your right knee with your right hand (Figs. 206 and 207). The last two moves are exactly the same as Moves 1 and 2 except that they are performed on the opposite side.

7. Shift back onto the left leg by bending into the knee, continuing to face the same direction (Fig. 208). This move is performed in the same manner as Move 3 except that the sides are reversed. After this, take a step in place and shift weight onto the right foot and "hold the ball" on the left side to return to the original position.

Continue with Moves 1 through 7 to repeat this form back and forth on each side.

Main points: The waist and shoulders must be turned together as one unit and face the same direction. The shoulders and arms must be relaxed and the very minimum of strength should be used to guide the arms through the movements. The elbow should never be fully extended and one must be careful not to overextend the arm during the push. The upper body should be kept vertical and you must not lean forward with the push. Also, your gaze should be kept on the index finger of the hand that is being pushed out. The arm movements of pushing out and brushing the knee are performed simultaneously. For this purpose, all movements should follow the turning of the waist and the shifting of weight in unison with slow and steady breathing so that all movements flow together as a smooth and continuous motion without pauses.

Effects: This form requires a little more effort than the previous form because it involves stepping back and forth in each direction. It is useful for improving circulation in the shoulders, elbows, spine, and knees, and is very helpful in preventing arthritis. Performing this one form repeatedly for up to half an hour can reduce pain in the joints and improve muscle tone over the whole body.

4. Stroke Wild Horse's Mane   野馬分鬃

Transition: Continue from Brush Knee and Push to come back onto the left foot after pushing out to the right with your left hand (Fig. 208). Begin turning to the left with your weight on the left foot. Pivot your right foot on the heel to point it forward. Then shift your weight over to your right foot. As you do this, sweep your left hand back down to the left with the palm turned down, and bring this hand around so it faces upward at the front of your lower abdomen on the right. At the same time turn your right hand so that the palm faces up and bring it up in an arc to the front of your chest on the right side. Thus your hands should face each other to "hold the ball" on the right side (Fig. 209).

Moves:

1.   Continue turning to the left and shift your weight completely over to your right foot. Bend into your right knee as it takes the weight and draw your left foot in toward your right with only the toes touching (Fig. 210).

Fig. 209   Fig. 210

Fig. 211   Fig. 212   Fig. 213

2. Take a big step out to the left, heel first, and move onto your left leg by bending your knee. Straighten out your right leg as you shift two-thirds of your weight over to your left foot. As you shift your weight, stroke your right hand down while raising your left hand out to the left. The right hand ends up in front of the right hip joint, facing down, and the left hand goes up to eye level and faces up at an angle. Your eyes should follow the movement of your left hand (Figs. 211–213).

3. Begin turning to the right as you shift your weight back to your right foot by bending into the knee. Pivot the left foot on the heel once the weight is off of it so that it points forward. Keep turning to your right as you shift your weight back over to your left foot by bending the left knee and straightening your right foot. As you turn and shift your weight, bring your left hand back toward yourself to the front of your chest on the left with the palm facing down. Also, turn the right hand so it faces up and bring it in front of the lower abdomen on the left side to "hold the ball" on the left side (Figs. 214 and 215).

4. Continue turning to the right and shift your weight completely over to your left foot. Bend your left knee as it takes weight and draw your right foot in toward your left so that only the toes are touching (Fig. 216).

5. Take a step with your right foot, heel first, and shift two-thirds of your weight onto it as you "stroke the horse's mane" with your left hand and extend your right hand (Figs. 217–219).

This move is exactly the same as Moves 2 and 3 except that it is performed on the opposite side.

Fig. 214 Fig. 215 Fig. 216

Fig. 217 Fig. 218 Fig. 219

6. Turn back to your left, shifting weight over to your left foot, and pivot the right foot on the heel to point it forward. Continue turning to your left as you shift your weight back onto the right foot, and bring the left foot, in toward the right. Bring your right hand back toward yourself to "hold the ball" on the right side as in the original position with your right hand on top and your left hand on the bottom (Figs. 220 and 221).

Continue with Moves 1 through 5 to repeat this form back and forth on each side.

Fig. 220   Fig. 221

Main points: While stroking the horse's mane, the upper body must be kept upright and the chest should be kept relaxed (so as to remain contained). Your center of gravity must be lowered along with the stroking motion. The hands should part smoothly as the leading arm reaches out. It is essential that the shifting of weight and the movements of the arms are coordinated with the breathing to flow smoothly and continuously.

Effects: In this form extending and straightening the back in the stroking move is emphasized. For this reason, it is helpful in correcting curvature of the spine. This form also serves to enhance the respiratory function. Stroke the Horse's Mane is therefore beneficial for spondylarthritis as well as respiratory and circulatory diseases. Furthermore, the turning movements of the waist strengthens the pelvic and abdominal muscles.

5. Grasp Peacock's Tail   攬雀尾

Transition: The beginning of this form is identical with Stroke Wild Horse's Mane. After stepping to the right, stroking down with the left hand and extending the right hand, "hold the ball" on the right side (Figs. 220 and 221). Keep turning your waist to your left as you shift your weight back onto your right leg and draw your left

Fig. 222   Fig. 223   Fig. 224

leg in toward the right so that only the
toes are touching the ground (Fig. 222).

Moves:

1. Take a big step out to the left, heel
first, and move onto your left leg by
bending the knee. Straighten out your
right leg as you shift two-thirds of your
weight over to your left foot. As you
shift your weight, stroke your right hand
down while extending your left hand to
the left. The right hand ends up in front
of the right hip joint, facing down, and
the left hand goes up to face level, facing
up at an angle. Your eyes should follow
the movement of your left hand (Figs.
223 and 224).

2. Shift your weight back onto your
right leg. (Keep facing the same direction)
Turn your hands so that the left hand
faces down and the right hand faces up
and extend both arms out to your left.
Your right hand should come next to the
left elbow (Fig. 225).

Fig. 225

3. As you shift your weight further back onto your right foot, turn your waist right to face forward. Along with this, bring both arms back in an arc past the abdomen. The right hand swings back up into position, facing left behind the head. The left hand only travels as far as the front of the right hip bone and faces in. Your gaze should be on the palm of the right hand (Fig. 226).

4. Turn back to your left and begin shifting your weight onto your left foot. Continue the movement of your arms in a circle back out to the left. Sweep your left hand out to just in front of your chest with the palm facing in. (Your left forearm should be almost horizontal.) At the same time, bring your right hand past your

Fig. 226   Fig. 227   Fig. 228

face and down to shoulder level so both hands face each other (Fig. 227).

5. Keep shifting your weight over to your left foot bending into the knee so two-thirds of your weight comes over it. As you do this, press the bottom of your right hand up against your left wrist so that your arms cross. Your gaze should remain on your right hand all through these movements (Fig. 228).

6. Turn your left hand to face down and separate your hands by sliding the right hand over the back of the left. Both hands should then be extended, facing down at an angle (Fig. 229).

7. Shift your weight back onto your right foot bending into the knee. (Keep facing the same direction) As you

Fig. 232

shift back, bring both hands back toward yourself in a descending arc to just in front of your lower abdomen. Keep your arms relaxed and bend your elbows gently. Look straight ahead into the distance (Figs. 230 and 231).

8. Shift your weight to the front onto the left foot, bending into the knee as you push forward with both hands. Your hands should rise in a gentle curve up to chest level as they push (Fig. 232).

9. Shift your weight back over to your right foot as you turn your waist toward your right. As your weight comes off your left foot, pivot it on the heel so the foot points forward. Along with this, sweep your right hand to your right in a motion

Fig. 229   Fig. 230   Fig. 231

Fig. 233   Fig. 234

Fig. 235   Fig. 236   Fig. 237

similar to Cloud Hands, but leave your left hand in about the same place. Thus, you stand facing forward with your arms extended to both sides at shoulder level with both hands facing down at an angle. Your gaze should follow your right hand as it sweeps out to the right (Figs. 233 and 234).

10. Shift your weight over onto your left foot as you keep turning to the right. After shifting completely onto the left foot, bending into the knee, draw your right foot in with only the toes touching the ground. As you do this, circle your right hand down and around to the front of your lower abdomen on the left side so the palm faces up. At the same time, bring your left hand back in front of your chest on the left side with the palm facing down. Thus you "hold the ball" on the left side. Keep looking to your right (Figs. 235 and 236).

11. Take a step with your right foot, heel first, and shift two-thirds of your weight onto it as you "stroke the horse's mane" with your left hand and extend your right hand (Figs. 237 and 238).

Fig. 240

Fig. 238   Fig. 239

The moves in Grasp Peacock's Tail which follow are exactly the same as Moves 2 through 10 except that they are performed on the opposite sides (Figs. 239–246).

Continue with Moves 1 through 10 and do the exact opposite sequence after it to repeat this form back and forth on each side.

Fig. 241   Fig. 242   Fig. 243

Fig. 244   Fig. 245   Fig. 246

Main points: The shoulders should remain relaxed while "stroking the horse's mane," and the arms should be moved together with the shifting of the weight onto the forward leg. Before getting in position to press both hands together, all the weight must first come over the back foot so that the front foot is completely relaxed. The movement of pressing the arms together should come from the waist along with the turning movement of the pelvis in the direction of the push. For this move to be done correctly, it is essential that exhaling, shifting weight, and pressing the hands are done in unison.

The upper body should remain straight and upright even after pushing in one direction with the "hand press." One should not lean backward or forward. An effort must be made to always keep the upper body upright through all the movements. In the push with both arms facing out, you must be careful not to lean forward or extend the arms too far. The movement of the arms should simply follow the shifting of the weight forward.

All movements must come from the waist and not from just the shoulders and arms. Moving from the waist enables you to keep the back straight and relax the shoulders. This way the arm movements are coordinated with the shifting and turning of the pelvis to become smooth and steady.

Effects: The whole body is exercised in Grasp Peacock's Tail and the respiratory and circulatory functions are enhanced. This form also serves to strengthen the internal organs as well as to keep all the joints in the body supple and strong. Practicing this form regularly prevents pain and inflammation in all the major joints including low back pain. This form is also beneficial for organic disorders such as ulcers and hypertension.

6.   Crouch and One Leg Stance   下式独立

Transition: After pushing to the right with both hands in the last form, begin turning your waist to the left and shift your weight back onto your left foot. Bend into your left leg and straighten your right leg. Once all your weight is off your right foot, pivot it around on the heel to point forward. As you turn to the left,

Fig. 247

Fig. 248

move both hands around in an arc (left hand up past the face and right hand down in front of abdomen) to extend both hands to the left with the palms facing down at a slant. The right hand should be next to the left elbow (Figs. 247 and 248).

Moves:

1.   Start turning back to the right as you shift your weight back onto the right foot. Bend into the right knee and straighten the left leg. As you do this, sweep both arms back in a circle to the right side. Bring the left hand down to the front of the lower abdomen on the right side and right hand up to shoulder level (Fig. 249).

Fig. 249

Fig. 250   Fig. 251

2. Once all the weight comes off the left foot, bring it in toward the right foot with the toes lightly touching the ground. At the same time, bring your left hand up from your lower abdomen past your chest and up to the front of your face with the palm facing in. As you do this, form a "hook" with your right hand by holding the tips of all five fingers together and pointing them down (Fig. 250).

3. Take a step to your left and shift your weight over onto your left foot, bending

Fig. 252   Fig. 253

into the left leg and straightening the right leg to place about two-thirds of your weight over the left foot. As you do this, push with your left hand (the palm faces down at an angle). The right hand which is held in a "hook" is kept extended to the side so that both arms are extended at shoulder level. Your gaze should be kept on your left hand as it passes in front of your face and is extended (Fig. 251).

4. Shift all your weight back onto your right foot and extend your left foot to crouch back as low as you are able without undue strain. Turn your waist ninety degrees to the right to face forward as you crouch back. Adjust the position of your feet for balance and keep both feet flat on the ground. As you begin to crouch down onto your right foot, draw a big circle back toward yourself with your left

Fig. 254

Fig. 255

hand. As soon as you begin this big circular movement, turn your left hand to face inward, and as it begins to move forward, turn the palm downward so the fingers point in the direction of the movement. Continue to hold your right hand in a "hook" and keep it extended out to your right side (Figs. 252–254).

5. Stand up and shift your weight forward onto your left foot as you turn your waist to face the left. As you stand up and shift your weight, your left hand should also rise and push (the palm faces forward and slightly down at an angle). As you rise, bring your right hand back down to your side just next to your right hip joint and invert the "hook" so that the fingers point up (Figs. 255 and 256).

Fig. 256

134

6. Keep moving in the same direction to stand straight up on your left foot while raising your right knee. As you do this, raise your right hand up to face level while keeping it bent at the elbow so that the right knee and elbow face each other. Make your right hand face upward at a slant as if you were holding something up. At the same time, bring your left hand down to your side in front of the left hip joint. Hold your left hand down as if pressing down on something. Your gaze should be on your raised right hand (Fig. 257).

7. Step back with the right foot, placing it behind and to the side of the left foot.

Switch to the same position on the opposite side by standing on your right foot and raising your left leg, bending it at the knee. The left elbow and knee must face each other in the same manner as the previous move. Also bring your right hand down in front of the right hip joint as you step onto your right foot as if you were pressing down. Your gaze should be shifted to your left hand (Fig. 258).

8. Bend your right leg a little and take a step to the left with your left foot, heel first. Then turn your waist to the right as you pivot your left foot on the heel so that it points

Fig. 257   *Fig. 258*

Fig. 259   *Fig. 260*

forward. Also adjust your right foot so that it points forward. At the same time as taking a step with your left foot, extend both hands to your left side at chest level (the right hand moves up while the left hand moves down). Your right hand should come next to the left elbow. As you turn around to the right, move both hands around to the right side in arcs (right hand moves up past the face and the left hand moves down past the lower abdomen) so that both hands face down at a slant and the left hand is next to the right elbow (Figs. 259 and 260).

9. Turn back to your left and shift your weight onto your left foot, bending into the knee. Bring both hands back around to the left side and start to form a "hook" with your left hand as you bring your right hand up past your lower abdomen to your face. Draw in your right foot toward your left with just the toes touching the ground. Then take a step with your right foot and push to the right with your right hand and continue to hold the "hook" with your left hand (Figs. 261–263).

Fig. 261

The moves in Crouch and One Leg Stance which follow are exactly the same as Moves 3 through 8 except that they are performed on the opposite sides (Figs. 264–271).

Continue with Moves 1 through 8 and do the exact opposite sequence after it to repeat this form back and forth on each side.

Fig. 262

Fig. 263

Fig. 264

Fig. 265

Main points: When crouching on one leg, you must not attempt to go any lower than your own limit. When standing in the one foot stance, the leg you are standing on should be slightly bent. The upper body must be kept vertical and there should be a brief pause before going on to the next move.

Fig. 266

Fig. 267

Fig. 268

Fig. 269   Fig. 270   Fig. 271

Effects: This form is particularly effective for improving circulation, increasing strength in the legs, and developing your sense of balance. Thus the Crouch and One Leg Stance is beneficial in cases of arthritis, gastroptosis, constipation, and neurasthenia.

7. Heel Kick   蹬脚

Transition: Continuing from the "one leg stance" with the right leg and right arm raised, take a big step to the right, heel first. Pivot your right foot on the heel to point it forward as you turn your waist ninety degrees to face forward (Fig. 271).

Shift all your weight over onto your right foot after this so that all your weight comes off the left foot and pivot it on the toes. As you take a step and turn to the left as described, bring your right hand down and around to the front of your lower abdomen on the right side and raise your left hand in front of your right shoulder to "hold the ball" on the right side (Fig. 272).

Fig. 272

Moves:

1. Just as in Move 1 of Brush Knee and Push, keep all your weight on the right leg and turn slightly back to face the right side. Raise your right arm by backtracking on the previous motion to move the hand out to the right at face level with the palm facing in. At the same time, press your left hand down in front of your lower abdomen. As you do this, your left foot should move in toward the right with the toes lightly touching the ground. Your gaze should be on the right index finger (Fig. 273).

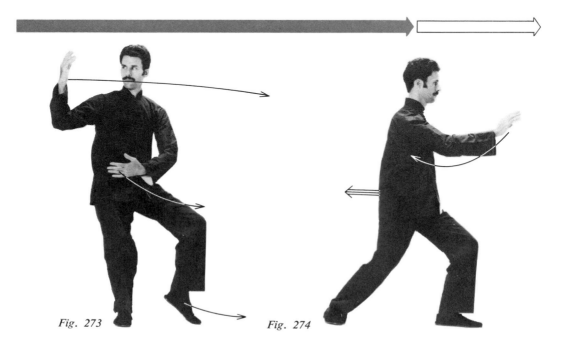

Fig. 273   *Fig. 274*

2. Proceed with Move 2 of Brush Knee and Push. Thus, turn to the left and take a big step, heel first. Continue to turn and shift two-thirds of your weight onto your left foot. As you turn and take a step, push your right hand to the left past your face and also brush over your left knee with your left hand. Your body should remain upright and your gaze should remain on the index finger of your right hand (Fig. 274).

3. Shift your weight back to your right foot and turn your waist back ninety degrees to face forward. As your weight comes off the left foot, pivot it on the heel along with the turn so that it points forward. Bend into your right leg and extend your left leg. As you do this, cross both arms in front of your chest so the right arm is over the left (Fig. 275).

4. Shift your weight back onto your left foot without turning your waist. Bend your left knee to bring all your weight over the left foot and straighten your right leg. As you do this, spread your arms out to both sides so that your hands face down at an angle (Fig. 276).

Fig. 275

Fig. 276

5. Lift your right foot and bring it in toward your left with the toes touching the ground. As you draw your right foot in, cross your arms in front of your chest in the same way as before (right arm over left). The extending and recrossing of the arms should draw an oblong circles out to both sides (Fig. 277).

6. Kick out with your right leg by first raising the knee up to waist level and then kicking up with your heel. As you kick, push forward with your right hand to fully extend it along with the raised leg and also raise your left hand over your head so the palm faces up at an angle (Fig. 278).

Fig. 277

Fig. 278

7. Put your right foot down toes first after the "heel kick" and bring your hands back in front of your abdomen to "hold the ball" on your left side (right hand on top and left hand on bottom: Fig. 279).

8. Continue the Brush Knee and Push sequence and duplicate the same moves from Moves 2 through 6 on the opposite side to "cross hands" at

Fig. 279

Fig. 280

Fig. 281

the wrist with the left arm over the right and do the "heel kick" to the left (Figs. 280–285).

Continue with Moves 1 through 6 and repeat the same sequence on the opposite side to do this form back and forth on each side.

Main points: You should stay in balance and kick only as high as you are able. Keeping your center of gravity low and concentrating on Dantian is important for staying in balance. The heel kick must be smooth and unstrained. The upper body should remain straight and upright as much as possible and must not lean forward or backward. For this purpose the kick should be at a ninety degree angle to the supporting foot. The foot must be planted firmly on the ground and the knee should be bent slightly for stability.

Effects: This Tai Chi form strengthens the muscles and tendons of the legs and pelvis and improves your sense of balance. It therefore effectively prevents aging

Fig. 282

Fig. 283

Fig. 284

Fig. 285

especially in the lower half of the body in addition to regulating the function of the central nervous system. The Heel Kick is also effective in curing and preventing problems in the lumbar and hip joints. The dynamic movements of this form are also useful for curing cases of neurasthenia.

8. Cross Hands 十字手

Transition: Continue on from a Heel Kick to the left and follow this with a Brush Knee and Push to the left. To do this sequence, put the left foot down toes first after the kick, keeping most of your weight on the right foot. At the same time bring your right hand down and around to the front of your lower abdomen and bring your left hand back in front of your chest to "hold the ball" on your right side (Fig. 286).

Fig. 286   Fig. 287   Fig. 288

Turn back to the right as your move your right hand back in an arc to your right side so it comes up to eye level and faces you. At the same time press your left hand down in front of your lower abdomen. Move your left foot in toward your right foot with the toes lightly touching the ground. Your gaze should be on your right index finger (Fig. 287).

Take a big step to the left, heel first, as you turn to the left. Continue to turn after taking the step to shift your weight onto your left foot by bending into the knee. As you take the step and turn, push your right hand to the left past the side of your head and also brush over your left knee with your left hand. This completes the Brush Knee and Push sequence to the left (Fig. 288).

Moves:

1. Turn back ninety degrees to the right to face forward and shift your weight evenly onto both legs to get into a half squatting stance, keeping your upper body upright. As you do this, cross your arms in front of your chest, bringing your right arm over your left (Fig. 289).

2. Shift all your weight over to your right foot and spread both arms out in an upward arc so that your hands face out (Fig. 290).

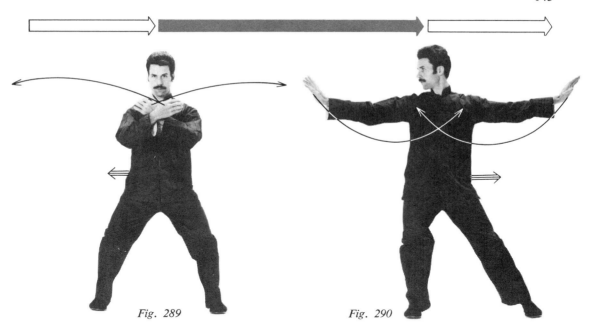

Fig. 289   Fig. 290

3. Shift your weight back over to your left foot and slide your right foot in toward the left so that your feet are about shoulder-width apart. Stand in the half squatting stance. As you do this, cross your arms once more in front of your chest with the right arm over the left (Fig. 291).
4. Stand up straight but leave your knees slightly bent as you raise both arms together past your face. Meanwhile turn the hands to face outward (Fig. 292).

Fig. 291   Fig. 292

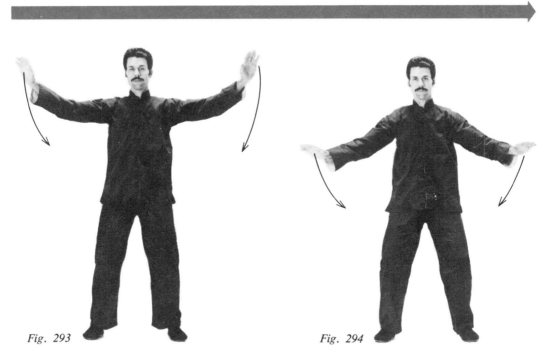

Fig. 293

Fig. 294

5. Keep raising both arms up over your head and turn your hands so they face out. Continue moving your arms down and around in big circles out to both sides (Fig. 293).

6. Squat down slowly as your arms begin to come down. By the time your arms come down and around to cross in front of your knees you should be in a deep squat with your thighs almost parallel with the ground. Both of your feet should remain flat

Fig. 295

Fig. 296

Fig. 297

Fig. 298   Fig. 299   Fig. 300

on the ground. Cross your arms slightly above and in front of your knees by
bringing the left arm over the right
(Figs. 294–297).

7. Begin to stand up as you raise
your crossed arms and turn your
hands to face inward as they come up
in front of your abdomen so that your
right arm comes over your left arm
(Figs. 298 and 299).

8. Stand up straight but leave your
knees slightly bent. Raise both arms
together up past your face and begin
turning the hands to face outward
(Fig. 300).

9. Keep raising your arms up over
your head and turn your hands out.
Continue moving them down and
around in big circles out to both sides
(Fig. 301).

Fig. 301

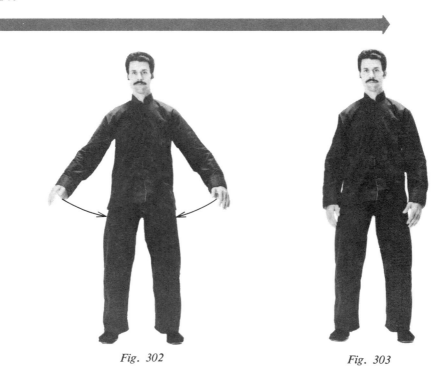

Fig. 302   Fig. 303

10.   This time, do not squat down as you lower your arms; instead just bring your arms down to your sides and relax them. You should be looking straight ahead into the distance (Figs. 302 and 303).

You may choose to do just one sequence of Cross Hands as described above, or you may slowly repeat Moves 6 through 8 as many times as you wish before going into Moves 9 and 10 to bring the series of Tai Chi exercises to a close.

Main points: The squatting motion and the circling of the arms must be synchronized with your breathing. You must exhale as the arms and body come down and inhale as the arms and body rise back up together. Both the breathing and movements must be slow and smooth. You must squat as deeply as you can while exhaling completely and keep the back as straight as possible. You should lean forward slightly and stick the hips out in order to keep the back straight. The heels must stay on the ground as you squat down. You should also inhale deeply while standing up and raising the arms.

Chapter 5

Qigong for Curing Diseases

Complementary Exercise and Therapy

Qigong can be readily combined with other forms of therapy to increase its therapeutic value and facilitate the healing process. Some exercises and treatments that can be effectively combined with Qigong are introduced in this chapter.

Remedial Exercise

It has been confirmed through clinical studies in China that an appropriate amount of calisthenic exercises practiced in conjunction with Qigong therapy compounds its benefits. Basically, Qigong exercises serve to improve the functional condition of internal organs, while calisthenic exercises primarily improve the condition of the skeletal muscles. Therefore, practicing both types of exercises improves the functional balance between the muscular system and the various organ systems, and this accelerates the recovery of health.

The therapeutic exercises recommended along with Qigong in the early days of modern Qigong therapy were simple remedial exercises that had existed in China for centuries. These remedial exercises originated from Taoist and Buddhist practices which were known to be very beneficial for attaining health and longevity. These exercises appeared to aid the recovery process of the patients to some extent, but these exercises were not systematized by exercise physiologists to suit the needs and tastes of people today, so they were in many instances too simple and repetitive. Therefore, people had a tendency of becoming bored with them and of giving them up. For this reason, initially the benefits derived from these remedial exercises were not as great as had been expected.

In order to have patients recovering from illnesses get more exercise in addition to Qigong, programs of light physical work like gardening, including the planting of seedlings and shrubs and the pulling of weeds, were assigned in Chinese rehabilitation centers. After more medical research had been done concerning the physiological effects of traditional remedial exercises, a simplified form of Tai Chi was introduced to patients undergoing Qigong therapy. It was found that the simplified Tai Chi exercise fits in very well with the Qigong therapy rehabilitation program. In addition to raising the level of interest among patients, the introduction of the simplified Tai Chi form increased the recovery rate noticeably. Thus it was confirmed that Tai Chi was a perfect therapeutic adjunct to Qigong.

From the clinical studies that have been conducted in China, it has been found that people with ulcers and other diseases which are complicated by psychological factors can benefit greatly from leisurely walks and light outdoor work such as gardening during the initial recovery period. Once people have shown a certain degree of improvement and have recovered some of their strength, slow moving exercises such as Tai Chi are ideal for facilitating complete rehabilitation. Tai Chi exercises also serve as prevention when they are practiced after complete recovery.

For the best results, this type of therapeutic exercise must be done on a regular basis, allowing a substantial amount of practice time for each session (about one hour). However, care must be taken not to overdo these exercises and not to become excessively fatigued. If a person is physically weak, the exercise session should include several short breaks. These breaks, however, should not be too long or too frequent as to interrupt the flow of the exercise. Also, the following points should be kept in mind when attempting to undertake a program of remedial exercise.

- Practice these exercises in a calm and carefree state of mind. Use the least amount of strength that you can and strive to make the movements flowing and graceful. Start off by learning the exercises with relatively simple movements and gradually progress to the more difficult exercises as you master the simple ones.
- The number of repetitions and the speed of performing these exercises should be adjusted according to your physical condition. Generally, when first learning these exercises, you should start by doing the exercises as slowly and carefully as you can with few repetitions. After mastering these exercises, the speed and number of repetitions can be progressively increased.
- You should routinely do some simple stretching and warm-up exercises before doing Tai Chi or other exercise routines. Also it is important to conclude each practice session with appropriate closing moves.
- Those who are unable to perform such exercises can do light manual labor within the limits of their ability. This includes light gardening tasks such as watering, weeding, and planting as well as simple household chores like sweeping, cleaning windows, and washing clothes. It is important that you do not exceed your physical capacity, but some exercise is an essential element in speeding up recovery. Even if a person is incapable of moving around, he can still contribute substantially to his own recovery by doing Preventive Qigong twice daily.

There are old Chinese proverbs which say, "Running water never goes bad" and "Hinges of well used doors never rust." These sayings emphasize that the body stays in good condition so long as it is exercised on a regular basis.

Complementary Therapy

Chemotherapy: The use of drugs is sometimes necessary to deal with the symptoms in some diseases. However, the use of drugs generally does nothing to increase a person's level of health and sometimes it is even detrimental to health. Therefore, one should begin practicing Qigong as soon as the symptoms have been reduced to a manageable level. The ideal thing would be to rely primarily on Qigong after partially recovering and to use drugs only as a last resort. Nevertheless, one must make sure in cases of serious illnesses that one's condition has truely stabilized so that medication is not discontinued prematurely.

Massage: When a person is unable to exercise due to an illness, injury, or a simple lack of energy, massage and other types of manipulation serve as an ideal substitute for remedial exercises. Massage, acupressure, and other forms of manipulation are an effective way to speed recovery so that a person can begin to exercise on his own. It is also possible to do a certain amount of massage and pressure point therapy on one's own, and this is generally encouraged in Qigong aside from the self-administered massage routines of Preventive Qigong. Naturally, it is better if one is able to receive treatments from another person, preferably from a professional. This will reinforce the effects of the self-help therapy that is being performed and otherwise such treatments enable and encourage a person to undertake a full Qigong exercise program as soon as possible.

Acupuncture: Receiving acupuncture treatments while undertaking Qigong therapy has been proven in China as being an excellent way to facilitate recovery from illness. At the Beidaihe Qigong Therapy Institute, one of the largest Chinese medical institutions researching Qigong therapy, in addition to Qigong therapy patients receive orthodox Western medical treatments as well as traditional Oriental remedies including herbs and acupuncture from specialists in each field. The widespread and effective use of acupuncture as an adjunct to Qigong therapy is a well accepted fact in the Chinese medical community.

Acupuncture provides prompt and effective relief from symptoms such as headaches and tension in the neck and shoulders, even though the causes may range from hypertention to dysfunctions of the autonomic nervous system. Acupuncture treatments on designated points generally alleviate such problems immediately, and also acupuncture can even lower the blood pressure in cases of hypertension. Acupuncture is also effective in providing prompt relief from pain caused by disorders of the digestive system such as ulcers and acute gastritis and can relieve discomfort in the stomach area, whatever the cause. Even in serious cases of paralysis caused by cerebro-vascular accidents, acupuncture is useful in reducing contracture in the joints and maintaining muscle tone. Japan is now following China's lead in using acupuncture for paralysis, and more and more hospitals are adopting acupuncture as a valuable tool for rehabilitation.

In this manner, acupuncture has proven effective for a wide variety of diseases, and most of the chronic diseases which respond to Qigong therapy are also treatable by acupuncture. Furthermore, acupuncture improves the health of those who are ill and strengthens those who are already healthy. One of the cardinal principles in acupuncture has always been to treat "incipient diseases," or to provide preventive care. The Chinese and people in the Far East have used acupuncture and remedial exercises for many centuries as a way of preventing disease and maintaining health and vigor. Qigong and acupuncture usually complement each other to increase the benefit of the other, and thus the salutary effect is compounded. It is unquestionable that acupuncture improves the circulation of Qi and works to restore the functional equilibrium of the body. The objective in Qigong therapy is essentially the same, but Qigong is an exercise working with both the mind and body on one's own. A powerful healing force is generated when physical therapy of massage or acupuncture is received from another person to effectively complement self-help therapy like Qigong.

Acupuncture is highly recommended especially for those who are serious about Qigong because the aid of an experienced therapist or acupuncturist is invaluable for increasing one's awareness of the dynamics of Qi, which can generate a powerful healing force. The next section lists the complementary therapy for individual diseases, and also provides an explanation about the effect of acupuncture treatments including the most effective points. This information may be used to decide the type of treatment and exercise program while recovering from a disease. The portion on acupuncture can also be used as reference in providing acupressure or heat stimulation to special points. It is always best, however, to consult a qualified acupuncturist to receive a complete diagnosis and treatment.

Qigong and Complementary Therapy for Various Diseases

The variety of disease recommended for treatment with Qigong has increased tremendously since it was first officially incorporated in the Chinese medical establishment as exercise therapy. Official studies released in 1966 show that it was used successfully to treat over eighty different diseases. The effectiveness of Qigong therapy, however, varies by the type of disease being treated. According to statistics from China, the average rate of effectiveness for the eighty diseases treated was over 85 percent. For diseases of the digestive system alone, the rate of effectiveness was 52 percent. Qigong is considered to be effective in about 90 percent of the cases for diseases of the respiratory, circulatory, endocrine, and reproductive systems. It is specially worth noting that the Chinese have had great success in treating chronic conditions like hypertension and diabetes with Qigong.

Qigong is also being used in China to treat cancer. However, research is still being done in this area, and the number of cases where complete recovery have been achieved are considerably less than for other diseases. While Qigong is quite effective against some types of cancer, it is ineffective against other types. It will take more time before the healing principles of Qigong in relation to cancer are scientifically established.

The recommendations for Qigong therapy and complementary exercise are listed individually for each type of disease in this section. It is most desirable that the Qigong practice be augmented with other forms of therapy such as massage and acupuncture.

Diseases of the Digestive System

Gastric and Duodenal Ulcers

Main Regimen:
Practice Inner Regulation Qigong. If one has a poor appetite or is thin, the Soft Breathing technique is recommended. If one has a good appetite, has hyperacidity, or is in great pain, the Hard Breathing technique is recommended. Those who are physically weak should practice in one of the lying postures. The seated postures may be used after regaining strength.

Practice four to six times a day for thirty minutes to an hour at a time. If working, a person should utilize the breaks at work to practice two or three times a day for a total of thirty minutes to an hour.

Complementary Exercise:
(1) Relaxation Qigong: Practice this exercise several minutes before beginning Inner Regulation Qigong as preparation.
(2) Preventive Qigong: Knocking Teeth, Swallowing Saliva, Waist Rotation, Dantian Rub
(3) Tai Chi

Acupuncture:
Many ulcers are a result of mental and physical stress, and acupuncture is generally very effective in alleviating symptoms of stress. Treating the hardened and tender points on the back including Geshu (B-17), Ganshu (B-18), and Pishu (B-20) provides pleasant stimulation which promotes mental and physical relaxation. Thus, the cause of the ulcer can be alleviated and the pain is reduced. Aside from the above mentioned points, often a hard spot appears in the back muscles just medial to the scapula around Gaohuang (B-43). Also, acupuncture stimulation of Renying (S-9), directly over the carotid sinus (a special technique developed by Dr. Bunshi Shirota of Japan), is known to have a dramatic effect in reducing pain associated with ulcers.

Gastroptosis

Main Regimen:
Practice Inner Regulation Qigong with either the Hard or Soft Breathing techniques. Use the supine position. In the case of gastroptosis, it is best to keep the feet raised a little higher than the head by placing some cushions below the legs, or by propping the foot of the bed up. Once the downward displacement of the stomach is nearly cured, one may use a preferred seated posture. Practice four to six times a day for thirty minutes to an hour at a time.

Complementary Exercise:
(1) Preventive Qigong: Knocking Teeth, Tongue Exercise, Waist Rotation, Dantian Rub
(2) Calisthenics: Sit-ups and push-ups
(3) Tai Chi

Acupuncture:
Acupuncture treatments are effective in alleviating the dull pain in the abdomen and back areas which often accompany gastroptosis. Also, acupuncture serves to improve the tonus of the smooth muscles of the stomach. It is important that the general tonification points be treated periodically aside from local points. Abdominal points include Qihai (CV-6), Shuifen (CV-9), Zhongwan (CV-12), Liangmen (S-21), Tianshu (S-25), and Zhangmen (Liv-13). Back points include Shenzhu (GV-12), Ganshu (B-18), Pishu (B-20), Weishu (B-21), and Weicang (B-50). The points Quchi (LI-11) and Zusanli (S-36) on the limbs are also used frequently. Otherwise, when there is tenderness in the epigastric region, Juque (CV-14) and Burong (S-19) are useful. Also, when there are psychosomatic symptoms such as headaches, dizziness, neck and shoulder tension, and general fatigue, the points Baihui (GV-20), Jianjing (G-21) and Tianzhu (B-10) are effective.

Chronic Gastritis

Main Regimen:
Practice Inner Regulation Qigong with either Hard or Soft Breathing. Those who have indigestion or a poor appetite, or those who are underweight should use Soft Breathing. Those who just have mild pain in the stomach but no digestive problems should use Hard Breathing. Concentrate on Dantian in both cases. Practice four to six times a day for thirty minutes to an hour at a time.

Complementary Exercise:
(1) Preventive Qigong: Arm Extension, Back Rub, Dantian Rub
(2) Tai Chi

Acupuncture:

Just as in the case of gastroptosis, an acupuncture treatment to remove muscular tension in the shoulder and back area is often effective in relieving the pain and discomfort of chronic gastritis. Geshu (B-17) and Ganshu (B-18) on the back, and Jianjing (G-21) on the shoulder are useful points. In cases where there is tenderness particularly around Pishu (B-20) on the left side, strong stimulation on this point is quite effective. Also the points Zhongwan (CV-12), Juque (CV-14), and Qimen (Liv-14) on the abdomen are indicated. The point Zusanli (S-36) is recommended for almost all digestive disorders, but for those with hyperacidity, Yanglingquan (G-34) should be used instead.

Chronic Constipation

Main Regimen:

Practice Inner Regulation Qigong using Soft Breathing. Concentrating on Dantian is important. Practice four to six times a day for thirty minutes to an hour at a time.

Complementary Exercise:
(1)   Relaxation Qigong
(2)   Preventive Qigong: Knocking Teeth, Swallowing Saliva, Dantian Rub
(3)   Tai Chi

Acupuncture:

People with chronic constipation often have accompanying symptoms such as distension in the lower abdomen, low back pain, headaches, or tension in the neck and shoulders. Acupuncture is generally very effective in alleviating such symptoms and usually bowel movements occur shortly after a treatment. The effective points for constipation located on the abdomen are Fushe (Sp-13), Tianshu (S-25), and Qihai (CV-6). The points on the back Shenshu (B-23) and Dachangshu (B-25), in addition to improving intestinal function, are also known to be effective for low back pain. There is another non-standard point which is specially effective for constipation. It is located on the left side of the lower back just above the highest point of the iliac crest. The acupuncture needle is inserted at a downward angle to directly stimulate the descending colon.

Pyloric Stenosis (due to ulcer)

Main Regimen:

Practice Inner Regulation Qigong using Hard Breathing. Practice in the supine position or the side-lying position on right side. Practice four to six times a day for thirty minutes to an hour at a time.

Complementary Exercise:
(1)   Preventive Qigong: Knocking Teeth, Tongue Exercise, Swallowing Saliva, Waist Rotation, Dantian Rub
(2)   Tai Chi

Intestinal Tuberculosis

Main Regimen:
Practice Inner Regulation Qigong with Soft Breathing. Concentrate on Dantian. Those who are weak should practice in a lying posture and use a seated posture after recovering strength. Those who are strong should practice mainly in the seated posture. Practice four to six times a day for thirty minutes to an hour at a time.

Complementary Exercise:
(1)   Preventive Qigong
(2)   Tai Chi

Post-gastrectomy Syndrome

Main Regimen:
Practice Inner Regulation Qigong with Hard Breathing. Concentrate on Dantian. Practice mainly in the supine and right side-lying positions, and occasionally in the seated postures. Practice four to six times a day for thirty minutes to an hour at a time.

Complementary Exercise:
(1)   Preventive Qigong

Chronic Enteritis

Main Regimen:
Practice Inner Regulation Qigong with Hard Breathing. Concentrate on Dantian. Those who are weak should practice mostly in lying postures and those who are strong should practice mainly in seated postures. Practice four to six times a day for thirty minutes to an hour at a time.

Complementary Exercise:
(1)   Preventive Qigong: Knocking Teeth, Tongue Exercise, Swallowing Saliva, Dantian Rub
(2)   Tai Chi

Acupuncture:
When received regularly over a long period, acupuncture treatments can reduce the

symptoms of enteritis substantially. The commonly used points on the abdomen include Zhongwan (CV-12), Liangmen (S-21), Tianshu (S-25), Daju (S-27), Huangshu (K-16), and Zhangmen (Liv-13). The points used on the back are Pishu (B-20), Shenshu (B-23), Dachangshu (B-25), and Zhongliao (B-33). On the limbs Quchi (LI-11), Zusanli (S-36), and Kunlun (B-60) are often used. When there is stomach pain, Liangqiu (Liv-34), Zhangmen (Liv-13), Zusanli (S-36), and Pishu (B-20) are indicated. When a person has been exposed to cold and has diarrhea, Zhogliao (B-33) should be acupunctured. In addition, Qihai (CV-6) and the point on the center of the soles should be heated, preferably by burning moxa cones. When there is constipation, Dachangshu (B-25) is effective in promoting bowel movements.

Chronic Appendicitis

Main Regimen:
Practice Inner Regulation Qigong with Hard Breathing. Concentrate on Dantian. Practice four to six times a day for thirty minutes to an hour at a time.

Complementary Exercise:
(1)   Preventive Qigong: Dantian Rub
(2)   Tai Chi

Acupuncture:
The dull pain which occasionally recurs on the right side of the lower abdomen can be relieved by acupuncture treatments. The points indicated on the abdomen are Qihai (CV-6), Fushe (Sp-13), Tianshu (S-25), and Daju (S-27) on only the right side. As for the back, Shenshu (B-23), Zhishi (B-52), and Dachangshu (B-25), as well as an extra point about one finger width to the outside of Dachangshu, are known to be effective. There is another extra point used in China for appendicitis called Lanwei which lies about 4 inches (10 centimeters) below Zusanli (S-36). When a person has appendicitis, there is usually a point that is very tender midway up the tibia on the outside. Strong acupuncture stimulation at this point is highly effective.

Chronic Indigestion

Main Regimen:
Practice Inner Regulation Qigong with Hard Breathing. Concentrate on Dantian. Use mainly the lying postures, especially the right side-lying position. Practice four to six times a day for thirty minutes to an hour at a time.

Complementary Exercise:
(1)   Preventive Qigong: Tongue Exercise, Swallowing Saliva, Waist Rotation, Dantian Rub
(2)   Tai Chi

Acupuncture:

Acupuncture can be highly effective for digestive problems. Indigestion is caused by a wide variety of factors such as systemic diseases, disorders in the digestive organs, and simple nervous distress. Whatever the cause, abnormal functioning of the digestive organs impair the body's ability to digest and assimilate food. Acupuncture treatments are initially directed toward improving the condition of the stomach, and therefore the points used are very similar to those used for chronic gastritis. They are Geshu (B-17), Ganshu (B-18), Pishu (B-20), and Jianjing (G-21) on the back, Zhongwan (CV-12), Juque (CV-14), and Qimen (Liv-14) on the abdomen, and naturally Zusanli (S-36) on the legs. Aside from these, Xiawan (CV-10), Sanyinjiao (Sp-6), Liangmen (S-21), and Sanjiaoshu (B-22) are effective for improving the appetite. When diarrhea is accompanied with lassitude or nausea, Baihui (GV-20), Shenshu (B-23), Fuliu (K-7), and Neiguan (P-6) are indicated.

Acute Hepatitis

Main Regimen:

Practice Inner Regulation Qigong with Soft Breathing. Concentrate on Dantian. Use either lying postures or seated postures. Practice three to four times a day for thirty minutes to an hour at a time.

Complementary Exercise:
(1)   Relaxation Qigong
(2)   Preventive Qigong
(3)   Stepping Qigong

Chronic Hepatitis

Main Regimen:

Practice Inner Regulation Qigong with Soft Breathing. Concentrate on Dantian. Use either lying postures or seated postures. Practice four to six times a day for thirty minutes to an hour at a time.

Complementary Exercise:
(1)   Preventive Qigong: Swallowing Saliva, Dantian Rub
(2)   Tai Chi

Acupuncture:

Regular acupuncture treatments can prove effective in alleviating the various symptoms of chronic hepatitis when continued over a long period. The main points used are Geshu (B-17), Ganshu (B-18), Danshu (B-19), and Jianjing (G-21) on the back, Zhongwan (CV-12), Zhangmen (Liv-13) and Qimen (Liv-14) on the abdomen, and Sanyinjiao (Sp-6), Yangligquan (G-34), Taichong (Liv-3), and Ququan (Liv-8) on the lower limbs.

Liver Cirrhosis

Main Regimen:
Practice Inner Regulation Qigong with Soft Breathing. Concentrate on Dantian. Use either lying postures or seated postures. Practice three to five times a day for thirty minutes to an hour at a time.

Complementary Exercise:
(1)   Relaxation Qigong
(2)   Vitalizing Qigong: Quiet Breathing in seated or standing postures; concentrate on Dantian.
(3)   Tai Chi

Cholecystitis

Main Regimen:
Practice Inner Regulation Qigong with Soft Breathing. Concentrate on Dantian. Use either lying of seated postures. Practice three to five times a day for thirty minutes to an hour at a time.

Complementary Exercise:
(1)   Relaxation Qigong
(2)   Preventive Qigong
(3)   Stepping Qigong

Acupuncture:
Mild cases of cholecystitis are treatable by acupuncture. The major points on the back are Geshu (B-17), Ganshu (B-18), Danshu (B-19), Geguan (B-46), Hunmen (B-47), and Yanggang (B-48), of which only the points on the right side are treated. The main points on the abdomen are Burong (S-19), Liangmen (S-21), Riyue (G-24), and Qimen (Liv-14), of which also only the right side is treated. Otherwise, Zhongwan (CV-12) and Yanglingquan (G-34) are indicated.

Diseases of the Circulatory System

Arteriosclerosis

In China heart diseases related to arteriosclerosis are separated into the five types discussed below. The amount and frequency of practice is the same for all heart diseases and circulatory disorders listed below. Practice three to five times a day for thirty minutes to an hour at a time.

Coronary Insufficiency

Subjective symptoms are not always present, but ECG readings taken in a resting state show clear signs of insufficient circulation to cardiac muscles.

Main Regimen:
Practice Vitalizing Qigong with Quiet Breathing. Concentrate on Dantian. Use either the standing or seated postures.

Complementary Exercise:
(1) Relaxation Qigong
(2) Preventive Qigong
(3) Tai Chi

Angina Pectoris

Main Regimen:
Practice Vitalizing Qigong with Quiet Breathing. Concentrate on Dantian. Use seated posture.

Complementary Exercise
(1) Relaxation Qigong
(2) Preventive Qigong
(3) Tai Chi

Acupuncture:
It is possible to reduce the acute symptoms of angina pectoris with acupuncture. Usually treatments are given after attacks to improve the condition of the heart and to prevent a relapse. Only mild acupuncture stimulation should be used. The following points are most often used: Tianzhu (B-10), Jueyinshu (B-14), and Xinshu (B-15) on the back; Shanzhong (CV-17), Shenfeng (K-23), and Shencang (K-25) on the left side of the chest; Shaohai (H-3), Tongli (H-5), Yinxi (H-6), and Ximen (P-4) on the arm. Also, Renying (S-9) may be used to stop an attack of angina pectoris.

Myocardial Infarction

This condition is marked by a circulatory obstruction in the coronary arteries. For sub-acute and chronic cases Qigong therapy is the same as for angina pectoris.

Myocardial Cirrhosis

This condition is marked by a loss of pulse along with hypertrophy and weakening of the heart. Qigong therapy is the same as for angina pectoris.

Arrhythmia

Subjective symptoms are often lacking in this condition also, but ECG readings clearly show abnormal heart beats.

Main Regimen:
Practice Vitalizing Qigong with Quiet Breathing. Concentrate on Dantian. Use seated posture.

Complementary Exercise:
(1)   Relaxation Qigong
(2)   Stepping Qigong

Hypertension

Main Regimen:
Practice Vitalizing Qigong with either Quiet Breathing or Deep Breathing. The inhalation should be short and the exhalation must be long. Use either the seated or standing postures. When using a seated posture, concentrate on Dantian. When practicing in a standing position, concentrate on Yongquan.

Complementary Exercise:
(1)   Relaxation Qigong
(2)   Preventive Qigong
(3)   Stepping Qigong
(4)   Tai Chi

Acupuncture:
Receiving regular acupuncture treatments over a period of time relieves the symptoms and stabilizes blood pressure. The commonly used point on the back are Tianzhu (B-10), Xinshu (B-15), Gaohuang (B-43), Fengchi (G-20), and Jianjing (G-21). Other useful points include Baihui (GV-20) on the top of the head, Shanzhong (CV-17) in the center of the chest, Quchi (LI-11) and Neiguan (P-6) on the arms, and Zusanli (S-36) and Yanglingquan (G-34) on the legs. Acupuncture stimulation of Renying (S-9) is also useful because it serves to reduce the blood pressure.

Essential Hypotension

Main Regimen:
Practice Inner Regulation Qigong with Hard Breathing. Concentrate on Dantian. Use either the lying or seated postures.

Complementary Exercise:
(1)   Preventive Qigong
(2)   Tai Chi

Acupuncture:

Regular acupuncture treatments over a period of time will relieve the symptoms and lead to improvement. The commonly used points on the back are Tianzhu (B-10), Xinshu (B-15), Geshu (B-17), Shenshu (B-23), Gaohuang (B-43), and Jianjing (G-21). On the abdomen Guanyuan (CV-4), Zhongwan (CV-12), and Shanzhong (CV-17) are used often. Points on the limbs such as Quchi (LI-11), Zusanli (S-36), and Sanyinjiao (Sp-6) are used often for general tonification along with Baihui (GV-20) on the head. People with hypotension tend to get chilled easily, and applying moxibustion on the center of the soles is remarkably effective for this.

Rheumatic Valvular Disease

Main Regimen:

Practice Inner Regulation Qigong with Soft Breathing. Concentrate on Dantian. Use either the lying or seated postures.

Complementary Exercise:

(1) Vitalizing Qigong: Deep Breathing in the seated posture, concentrating on Dantian.
(2) Preventive Qigong
(3) Stepping Qigong
(4) Tai Chi

Acupuncture:

With the exception of very serious cases, acupuncture is effective for symptomatic relief. The following points are indicated: Dazhu (B-11) and Xinshu (B-15) on the back; Juque (CV-14), Shanzhong (CV-17), and Shencang (K-25) on the front; Shenmen (H-7), Shaoze (SI-1), and Ximen (P-4) on the arms; Zusanli (S-36) on the legs.

Myocarditis

Main Regimen:

Practice Vitalizing Qigong with Quiet Breathing. Concentrate on Dantian. Use one of the lying postures.

Complementary Exercise:

(1) Preventive Qigong
(2) Tai Chi: Start with the Eight Basic Forms, and after becoming physically fit, learn and practice the more advanced forms.

Acupuncture:

Acupuncture is contra-indicated in acute cases, but it is beneficial in chronic cases. The effective points are Dazhu (B-11) and Xinshu (B-15) on the back, Shencang (K-25) on the chest, and Shaoze (SI-1) and Ximen (P-4) on the arms.

Raynaud's Disease

Main Regimen:
Practice Vitalizing Qigong with Quiet Breathing. Concentrate on Dantian. Use the seated posture.

Complementary Exercise:
(1) Relaxation Qigong
(2) Preventive Qigong
(3) Stepping Qigong
(4) Tai Chi

Acupuncture:
Acupuncture can be effective in the early stages of Raynaud's disease. Those points which are tender on the shoulders and arms are treated. In some cases there are specially effective tender points on the neck and head. Acupuncturing Renying (S-9) to reach the carotid sinus can also be quite effective.

Thrombophlebitis

Main Regimen:
Practice Inner Regulation Qigong with Soft Breathing. Concentrate on the soles of the feet (Yishou Jiaoji). Use either the lying or seated postures.

Complementary Exercise:
(1) Relaxation Qigong
(2) Stepping Qigong
(3) Tai Chi

Rheumatism

Main Regimen:
Practice Inner Regulation Qigong with either Soft or Hard Breathing. Concentrate on Dantian. Use both the lying and seated postures alternately.

Complementary Exercise:
(1) Preventive Qigong
(2) Stepping Qigong
(3) Tai Chi

Acupuncture:
Acupuncture is highly recommended in cases of rheumatism, and it is especially effective in the acute stage. Even after the symptoms become worse, acupuncture is effective in relieving the pain. When there is pain and inflammation in the joints

during the early stages of this disease, acupuncture stimulation of Renying (S-9) over the carotid sinus can be particularly effective. It is not unusual for pain in the right side of the body to disappear completely after acupuncturing Renying on the right side. Stimulating the carotid sinus on either side alternately on different occasions has a cumulative therapeutic effect.

Generally when there is redness, swelling, inflammation, and pain in the joints, strong acupuncture stimulation should be avoided. Using very fine acupuncture needles to make very shallow insertions in the painful sites is the most effective way to relieve the pain. Even leaving the needles inserted for a short time is often too much stimulation so quick insertion and quick withdrawal is necessary. The main tonification points should also be treated to improve the general condition. Points such as Baihui (GV-20) on the head, Tianzhu (B-10), Xinshu (B-15), Pishu (B-20), Shenshu (B-23), Dachangshu (B-25), Gaohuang (B-43), and Jianjing (G-21) on the back, Qihai (CV-6) and Zhongwan (CV-12) on the abdomen, and Quchi (LI-11), Sanyinjiao (Sp-6), Zusanli (S-36), and Yanglingquan (G-34) on the limbs are used.

Diseases of the Nervous System

Neurasthenia

Main Regimen:
Practice Vitalizing Qigong with either Quiet or Deep Breathing. Concentrate on Dantian. Use either the sitting or standing postures. Practice two or three times a day for thirty minutes to an hour at a time.

Complementary Exercise:
(1) Relaxation Qigong: Perform for several minutes prior to practicing Vitalizing Qigong.
(2) Inner Regulation Qigong: Soft Breathing in lying or sitting postures
(3) Preventive Qigong: Perform a few or all exercises after finishing the Passive Qigong regimen.
(4) Tai Chi

Acupuncture:
Often dramatic results can be obtained through continued acupuncture treatments. People with neurasthenia usually have many physical complaints such as headaches, insomnia, eyestrain, neck and shoulder tension as well as general fatigue. These people often have many tender points on their body, and treating these points, wherever they are, generally yields good results. Also, tonification points are commonly used as follows: Baihui (GV-20) on the head, Shenzhu (GV-12), Tianzhu (B-10), Xinshu (B-15), Shenshu (B-23), Gaohuang (B-43), and Jianjing (G-21) on the back, Quchi (LI-11) and Ximen (P-4) on the arms, and Sanyinjiao (Sp-6), Zusanli (S-36), and Yanglingquan (G-34) on the legs. Moxibustion or heat stimulation on Baihui is also very effective for neurasthenia.

Hysteria (Nervous Breakdown)

Main Regimen:
Guided Qigong Exercises are used. (This type of Qigong is not covered in this book. Since patients with hysteria are very susceptible to suggestions, Qigong exercises are performed under the guidance of specialists.)

Complementary Exercise:
(1)   Inner Regulation Qigong: Soft Breathing is used in the lying or seated postures. The repetition of an appropriate phrase for self-suggestion is especially effective for such people.
(2)   Vitalizing Qigong: Quiet Breathing in a seated posture

Gastric Neurosis

Main Regimen:
Practice Inner Regulation Qigong with Soft Breathing in the lying or seated postures. Practice three or four times a day for thirty to forty minutes at a time.

Complementary Exercise:
(1)   Preventive Qigong: Tongue Exercise, Swallowing Saliva, Dantian Rub
(2)   Stepping Qigong
(3)   Tai Chi

Acupuncture:
This is a condition for which acupuncture is particularly effective. For symptoms such as stomach pain, a feeling of distension in the abdomen, nausea, vomiting, and diarrhea, the points mentioned in the section for digestive disorders should be used according to the symptoms. Also, the general tonification points listed above for neurasthenia are used. Aside from this, acupuncturing Renying (S-9) provides quick relief from the strong abdominal pain associated with gastrospasms.

Cardiac Neurosis

Main Regimen:
Practice Vitalizing Qigong with Quiet Breathing in a seated posture. Practice four to six times a day for thirty minutes to an hour at a time.

Complementary Exercise:
(1)   Relaxation Qigong
(2)   Inner Regulation Qigong: Hard Breathing (keeping the pauses between breaths short) in a seated posture. Concentrate on Dantian.
(3)   Stepping Qigong
(4)   Tai Chi

Acupuncture:

The attacks and symptoms of cardiac neurosis can be alleviated by acupuncture in many cases. The first point to treat is Juque (CV-14) and Shanzhong (CV-17). Otherwise, one should look for tender spots between these two points to provide strong stimulation on this tender point. Also, the points Shaoze (SI-1) and Ximen (P-4) should receive extended acupuncture stimulation. Further, light stimulation at Xinshu (B-15) and Gaohuang (B-43) on the left side is useful.

Multiple Neuritis

Main Regimen:
Practice Inner Regulation Qigong using Soft Breathing. Concentrate on Dantian. Practice four or five times a day for thirty minutes to an hour at a time.

Complementary Exercise:
(1) Preventive Qigong
(2) Stepping Qigong
(3) Tai Chi

Acupuncture:
For cases caused by a deficiency of thiamine (vitamin B_1) or diabetes, acupuncture treatments can be effective. Those areas of the body which have pain, numbness, or motor impairment should be acupunctured directly for the best results.

Progressive Muscular Dystrophy

Main Regimen:
Preventive Qigong, practiced regularly, helps maintain a basic level of muscular strength and helps to inhibit the progress of the disease. Practice four to six times a day for about thirty minutes.

Complementary Exercise:
(1) Stepping Qigong
(2) Tai Chi

Myelitis

Main Regimen:
Practice Inner Regulation Qigong using Soft Breathing. Concentrate on Dantian. Practice four to six times a day for thirty minutes to an hour at a time.

Complementary Exercise:
(1) Preventive Qigong
(2) Tai Chi

Autonomic Ataxia

Main Regimen:

Practice Vitalizing Qigong with Quiet Breathing in either the lying or seated postures. Concentrate on Dantian. Practice four or five times a day for thirty minutes to an hour at a time.

Complementary Exercise:

(1) Inner Regulation Qigong: Use Soft and Hard Breathing techniques alternately in lying and seated postures.
(2) Preventive Qigong
(3) Stepping Qigong
(4) Tai Chi

Acupuncture:

Good results can be expected in the treatment of autonomic ataxia through acupuncture. Receiving treatments on a regular basis will serve to alleviate a wide variety of complaints including insomnia, headaches, neck and shoulder tension, nausea, a feeling of distension in the abdomen, hotness in the face, irritability, and chilling of the extremities. As for the selection of points, the general tonification points are used along with those for alleviating the existing symptoms.

The commonly used points are as follows: Baihui (GV-20) on the head, Tianzhu (B-10) and Jianjing (G-21) on the neck and shoulders, Xinshu (B-15), Geshu (B-17), Ganshu (B-18), Pishu (B-20), Shenshu (B-23), Dachangshu (B-25), Ciliao (B-32) and Gaohuang (B-43) on the back, Shanzhong (CV-17) on the chest, Qihai (CV-6) and Zhongwan (CV-12) on the abdomen, Quchi (LI-11) on the arms, and Sanyinjiao (Sp-6), Zusanli (S-36), Kunlun (B-60), and Yanglingquan (G-34) on the legs.

Sequela of Apoplexy (After-effects of Stroke)

Main Regimen

Practice Vitalizing Qigong with Quiet Breathing in a seated posture. Concentrate on Dantian. Practice four or five times a day for thirty minutes to an hour at a time.

Complementary Exercise:

(1) Preventive Qigong
(2) Stepping Qigong (for those who are able)
(3) Tai Chi (for those who are able)

Acupuncture:

Overcoming the after-effects of a stroke is a slow process and generally acupuncture treatments are required over a long period, but sometimes unexpectedly good results can be obtained. The sites where there is hardness in the muscles or rigidity in the joints should be acupunctured directly for the best results. It is also important to treat the general tonification points listed below.

Baihui (GV-20) on the head; Tianzhu (B-10), Fengchi (G-20), and Jianjing (G-21) on the neck and shoulders; Shenzhu (GV-12), Xinshu (B-15), Shenshu (B-23), Dachangshu (B-25), and Gaohuang (B-43) on the back; Qihai (CV-6), Zhongwan (CV-12), and Tianshu (S-25) on the abdomen; Hegu (LI-4), Shousanli (LI-10), and Quchi (LI-11) on the arms; Zusanli (S-36), Yanglingquan (G-34) and Zhongfeng (Liv-4) on the legs.

Cerebral Arteriosclerosis

Main Regimen:
Practice Vitalizing Qigong with Quiet Breathing in a seated posture. Concentrate on Dantian. Practice three or four times a day for thirty minutes to an hour at a time.

Complementary Exercise:
(1) Preventive Qigong: Eye Exercise, Ear Exercise, Back Rub
(2) Stepping Qigong
(3) Tai Chi

Acupuncture:
A preventive and beneficial effect can be expected when acupuncture treatments are received regularly. The commonly used points are as follows: Baihui (GV-20) on the head, Dazhui (GV-14), Fengchi (G-20), and Jianjing (G-21) on the neck and shoulders, Xinshu (B-15), Ganshu (B-18), Shenshu (B-23), and Gaohuang (B-43) on the back, Qihai (CV-6), Zhongwan (CV-12), and Juque (CV-14) on the abdomen, and Quchi (LI-11) and Zusanli (S-36) on the upper and lower limbs respectively.

Vascular Headache (Migraine)

Main Regimen:
Practice Vitalizing Qigong with Quiet Breathing in a seated posture. Concentrate on Dantian. Practice three to five times a day for thirty minutes to an hour at a time.

Complementary Exercise:
(1) Relaxation Qigong
(2) Preventive Qigong
(3) Stepping Qigong

Acupuncture:
Migraine headaches are treatable by acupuncture, and often the results are dramatic. Many of the points used are on the head, and they are selected according to the location of the pain. Also, aside from standard points such as Taiyang (extra), Baihui (GV-20), Tianzhu (B-10), and Fengchi (G-20), when the pain is in the back of the head, Weizhong (B-40) and Kunlun (B-60) are used, when the pain is in the side of the head, Yanglingquan (G-34) and Zulinqi (G-41) are used, and when the pain is in the front of the head, Shousanli (LI-10) and Zusanli (S-36) are used.

Diseases of the Respiratory System

Pulmonary Tuberculosis

Main Regimen:
In cases of active tuberculosis practice Vitalizing Qigong with Quiet Breathing in a seated posture. In cases of inactive tuberculosis practice Inner Regulation Qigong with Hard Breathing in a seated posture and occasionally in a lying posture. Practice four to six times a day for thirty minutes to an hour at a time.

Complementary Exercise:
Those with active tuberculosis should practice Preventive Qigong. Those with inactive Qigong should practice a few forms from the Eight Simplified Tai Chi Forms.

Acupuncture:
Before there were antibiotics to treat tuberculosis, many patients in the Far East were cured by acupuncture and moxibustion alone. Even today, acupuncture and moxibustion are useful in cases of tuberculosis as therapy to strengthen the physical constitution. The most effective method is to use moxibustion or to provide mild heat stimulation to selected points. The points used are Lingtai (GV-10), Shenzhu (GV-12), Zhongwan (CV-12), Chize (L-5), Zusanli (S-36), Dazhu (B-11), and Fengmen (B-12). The treatment should be started cautiously by first treating only Shenzhu and Fengmen. If the fever does not become worse, the points Lingtai and Chize may be added, and if this also produce no adverse reaction, Zhongwan and Zusanli can be added. Once the patient becomes accustomed to moxibustion treatments, other points can be added for symptomatic relief.

Acupuncture is also used to provide relief from symptoms, but care must be taken to keep the stimulation from becoming excessive. It is best to insert the needles very shallowly and not to leave them inserted. The points Chize, Dazhu, Renying (S-9), and Shufu (K-27) are used for quieting coughs. To provide relief from shoulder tension and pain in the back area, the points Fengmen, Xinshu (B-15), Jianjing (G-21), and Tianliao (TE-15) are used. To improve the appetite, Zhongwan (CV-12), Liangmen (S-21), Geshu (B-17), Pishu (B-20), and Weicang (B-50) are used. Aside from this, Baihui (GV-20), Shenmen (H-7), Tianzhu (B-10), Xinshu, Gaohuang (B-43), Wangu (G-12), and Fengchi (G-20) are used when a person is in a very emaciated condition or is having difficulty in getting sleep.

Chronic Bronchitis

Main Regimen:
Practice Inner Regulation Qigong with Soft Breathing. Concentrate on Dantian. Alternate between the lying and seated postures. Practice four to six times a day for thirty minutes to an hour at a time.

168

Complementary Exercise:
Tai Chi

Acupuncture:
Acupuncture and moxibustion treatments are useful and sometimes proves to be dramatically effective. Acupuncturing Renying (S-9) is a very effective way to quiet coughing spells along with the extra point Dingchuan (half an inch or one centimeter on either side of GV-14). Other effective points include Juque (CV-14), Tiantu (CV-22), Chize (L-5), Dazhu (B-11), Fengmen (B-12), Feishu (B-13), Yuzhong (K-26), Yifeng (TE-17), and Qimen (Liv-14). Otherwise, as general tonification points, Qihai (CV-6), Zhongwan (CV-12), Quchi (LI-11), Tianshu (S-25), and Zusanli (S-36) are often used. The points Lingtai (GV-10), Shenzhu (GV-12), Fengmen, and Yuzhong are particularly effective when moxibustion or heat stimulation is applied.

Bronchiectasis

Main Regimen:
In light cases, the regimen for bronchitis should be followed. In heavy cases, the regimen for pulmonary tuberculosis should be followed.

Complementary Exercise:
(1) Preventive Qigong
(2) Tai Chi

Acupuncture:
In many cases, acupuncture serves as an aid to recovery by alleviating the symptoms such as coughing and the production of phlegm, and by strengthening the constitution of the patient. The main points used are Chize (L-5), Renying (S-9), Dazhu (B-11), Fengmen (B-12), and Yuzhong (K-26). Otherwise, the general tonification points listed for bronchitis are used. Moxibustion is also very useful in the treatment of bronchiectasis and a few points on the Governor and Conception Vessels as well as on the Gallbladder Meridian are selected for treatment in this case. It is important to keep the heat stimulation relatively mild.

Pulmonary Silicosis

Main Regimen:
Practice Inner Regulation Qigong with Soft Breathing. If pausing the breath is difficult, Vitalizing Qigong with Quiet Breathing may be practiced instead. Use the seated and lying postures alternately. Practice four to six times a day for thirty minutes to an hour at a time.

Complementary Exercise:
Preventive Qigong

Bronchial Asthma

Main Regimen:
Practice Inner Regulation Qigong with Soft Breathing. Those with a very severe case may practice Vitalizing Qigong with Quiet Breathing. Use the seated and lying postures alternately. Practice four or five times a day for thirty minutes to an hour at a time.

Complementary Exercise:
(1)   Preventive Qigong
(2)   Tai Chi

Acupuncture:
Acupuncture and moxibustion give good results in cases of asthma. Acupuncturing Renying (S-9) is very useful as an emergency measure during asthma attacks. In this case, a thin gauge needle is inserted very shallowly to just reach the carotid sinus and then it is withdrawn immediately. The extra point Dingchuan, next to Dazhui (GV-14), is also specially effective for asthma. Aside from this, Xinhui (GV-22), Chize (L-5), Tianzhu (B-10), Dazhu (B-11), Fengmen (B-12), Feishu (B-13), Weicang (B-50), and Shufu (K-27) are used for chronic cases.

Bronchopneumonia

Follow the regimen and complementary exercises listed for asthma.

Emphysema

Follow the regimen and complementary exercises listed for asthma.

Blood Diseases

Iron Deficiency Anemia

Main Regimen:
Practice Inner Regulation Qigong with Hard Breathing. Concentrate on Dantian. Use the lying and seated postures alternately.

Complementary Exercise:
(1)   Vitalizing Qigong: Quiet Breathing in the cross-legged position
(2)   Stepping Qigong
(3)   Tai Chi

Acupuncture:
Although dietetic therapy is most important, in many cases acupuncture and

moxibustion can also be helpful. It has been shown in scientific studies that moxibus-tion substantially increases the amount of hemoglobin and the blood cell count. For this reason, moxibustion is the main treatment prescribed and acupuncture serves as an adjunct. Generally, moxibustion and various forms of heat stimulation are applied on the following points: Baihui (GV-20) on the head; Shenzhu (GV-12), Fengmen (B-12), Pishu (B-20), and Shenshu (B-23) on the back; Qihai (CV-6) and Zhongwan (CV-12) on the abdomen; Quchi (LI-11) on the arms, and Zusanli (S-36) and Zhao-hai (K-6) on the legs. The main points used for acupuncture are Xinshu (B-15), Ganshu (B-18), Pishu (B-20), and Sanjiaoshu (B-22) on the back, and Ximen (P-4) on the arms.

Aplastic Anemia

Main Regimen:
Practice Vitalizing Qigong. Concentrate on Dantian. Use the lying and seated postures alternately. Choose the breathing method according to the symptoms.

Complementary Exercise:
(1)   Preventive Qigong
(2)   Tai Chi

Diseases of the Excretory and Reproductive Systems

Chronic Cystitis

Main Regimen:
(1)   Vitalizing Qigong: Quiet Breathing using a seated posture
(2)   Inner Regulation Qigong: Soft or Hard Breathing using a lying posture
Concentrate on Dantian.

Complementary Exercise:
(1)   Preventive Qigong: Back Rub, Dantian Rub, Yongquan Massage, Leg Stretch
(2)   Stepping Qigong

Acupuncture:
Symptomatic relief from bladder dysfunctions such as polyuria (frequent urination) can be obtained through acupuncture and moxibustion. The main points used in acupuncture are Shenshu (B-23), Ciliao (B-32), and Zhongliao (B-33) on the lower back and hip area, as well as Zhongji (CV-3) and Dahe (K-12) on the lower abdomen. The points used for moxibustion include those used for iron deficiency anemia as well as Zhishi (B-52) on the back, Shuifen (CV-9), Daju (S-27) and Huangshu (K-16) on the lower abdomen, and Taixi (K-3) and Ququan (Liv-8) on the legs.

Chronic Nephritis

Follow the regimen and complementary exercises listed for cystitis. Acupuncture is also effective.

Prostatitis

Follow the regimen and complementary exercises listed for cystitis. Acupuncture is also effective.

Impotence

Main Regimen:
(1) Inner Regulation Qigong: Hard Breathing in a seated posture
(2) Vitalizing Qigong: Quiet Breathing in a seated posture

Complementary Exercise:
Preventive Qigong: Back Rub, Dantian Rub, Yongquan Massage, and Leg Stretch.

Acupuncture:
Cases of impotence caused by organic disorders cannot be helped, but acupuncture can prove remarkably effective for functional disorders caused by nervous conditions, overwork, or debility after an illness. The following points are most commonly used: Baihui (GV-20) on the head; Tianzhu (B-10) and Jianjing (G-21) on the neck and shoulders; Xinshu (B-15), Ganshu (B-18), Pishu (B-20), Shenshu (B-23), Ciliao (B-32), Zhongliao (B-33), Gaohuang (B-43), and Zhishi (B-52) on the back; Quchi (LI-11) and Ximen (P-4) on the arms, and Zusanli (S-36) and Sanyinjiao (Sp-6) on the legs.

Spermatorrhea (Excessive Emission)

Follow the regimen and complementary exercises listed for impotence. Acupuncture is also effective.

Diseases of the Endocrine System

Hyperthyroidism (Basedow's Disease)

Main Regimen:
Practice Vitalizing Qigong with either Quiet or Deep Breathing. Practice three to five times a day for thirty minutes to an hour at a time.

Complementary Exercise:
(1) Preventive Qigong
(2) Stepping Qigong

Acupuncture:
In light cases of hyperthyroidism, acupuncture and moxibustion can be fairly effective in reducing the symptoms. Acupuncturing Renying (S-9) is very effective along with skin-deep insertions around the thyroid gland. Otherwise, the commonly used points are as follows: Futu (LI-18) and Shuitu (S-10) on the throat, Tianzhu (B-10) and Fengchi (G-20) on the back of the neck, and Shenshu (B-23) and Zhishi (B-52) on the lower back. Moxibustion or heat stimulation on the above points is also effective.

Diabetes

Main Regimen:
(1) Inner Regulation Qigong: Soft Breathing using the seated and lying postures alternately
(2) Vitalizing Qigong: Quiet Breathing or Deep Breathing using the seated and standing postures alternately
    Practice either of these exercises two or three times a day for thirty minutes to an hour at a time.

Complementary Exercise:
(1) Preventive Qigong
(2) Stepping Qigong
(3) Tai Chi

Acupuncture:
In many cases, acupuncture and moxibustion are useful in the treatment of diabetes, and good results can be expected when used in combination with conventional medical care and dietetic therapy. The commonly used points on the back are Ganshu (B-18), Pishu (B-20), Sanjiaoshu (B-22), Shenshu (B-23), and Dachangshu (B-25) as well as Hunmen (B-47) and Yishe (B-49) on the left side. Otherwise, on the abdomen, Zhongwan (CV-12), Liangmen (S-21), Guanmen (S-22), and Fu-ai (Sp-16), on the left side especially, are used. In addition, Quchi (LI-11), Sanyinjiao (Sp-6), and Zusanli (S-36) are often used. When a patient has excessive thirst, Lianquan (CV-23) and Neiguan (P-6) may be added. Also, for symptoms of insomnia or dull headaches, heat stimulation on Baihui (GV-20) and acupuncture on Tianzhu (B-10) may be added.

Gynecological Diseases

Uterine Inflammation

This condition also includes inflammation of the uterine tubes and the peritoneum.

Main Regimen:
Practice Inner Regulation with either Hard or Soft Breathing. Concentrate on Dantian. In the beginning practice mostly in a lying posture, and later on, practice mostly in a seated posture. Practice four or five times a day for thirty minutes to an hour at a time.

Complementary Exercise:
Preventive Qigong: Shoulder Massage, Back Rub, Sacral Rub, Dantian Rub, Yongquan Massage, Leg Stretch

Acupuncture:
Acupuncture treatments are effective in providing symptomatic relief, and symptoms such as abdominal pain and distension as well as low back pain can be alleviated. The main points used are Shenzhu (GV-12), Shenshu (B-23), Dachangshu (B-25), Xiaochangshu (B-27), Ciliao (B-32), and Zhongliao (B-33) on the back, Zhongji (CV-3), Zhongwan (CV-12), Daju (S-27), and Dahe (K-12) on the abdomen, Quchi (LI-11) on the arms, and Sanyinjiao (Sp-6), Xuehai (Sp-10), and Zusanli (S-36) on the legs. When there is a dull headache or insomnia, the points Baihui (GV-20), Tianzhu (B-10), Wangu (G-12), and Jianjing (G-21) may be added.

Functional Uterine Bleeding

Main Regimen:
Practice Vitalizing Qigong with Quiet Breathing in a lying posture. Concentrate on Shanzhong.

Complementary Exercise:
Preventive Qigong: Back Rub, Dantian Rub, Leg Stretch

Acupuncture:
In some cases, acupuncture can prove very effective. The points specially effective for uterine bleeding are Shenshu (B-23), Xiaochangshu (B-27), and Ciliao (B-23) on the lower back, Zhongwan (CV-12) and Daju (S-27) on the abdomen, and Sanyinjiao (Sp-6) and Yanglingquan (G-34) on the legs.

Primary Amenorrhea

Main Regimen:
Vitalizing Qigong with Quiet Breathing in either the sitting or standing postures. Concentrate on Dantian.

Complementary Exercise:
(1) Preventive Qigong: Back Rub, Sacral Rub, Dantian Rub, Leg Stretch
(2) Stepping Qigong: Striking Dantian
(3) Tai Chi

Acupuncture:
Good results can be obtained with acupuncture. The points used are similar to those used for uterine inflammation. In cases where there are headaches and neck and shoulder tension, the points Baihui (GV-20), Tianzhu (B-10), and Jianjing (G-21) may be added.

Dysmenorrhea

Main Regimen:
Practice Inner Regulation Qigong with Soft Breathing, using the lying and seated postures alternately. Practice three times a day for thirty minutes to an hour each time.

Complementary Exercise:
Preventive Qigong: Back Rub, Sacral Rub, Yongquan Massage, Leg Stretch

Acupuncture:
Substantial results can be obtained with acupuncture and moxibustion. The main points used are similar to those used for uterine inflammation. Among these points, Daju (S-27), Dachangshu (B-25), Xiaochangshu (B-27), Ciliao (B-32), and Dahe (K-12) are particularly effective for dysmenorrhea. Receiving treatments one week prior to the start of menses usually prevents most of the symptoms. Also, moxibustion on Sanyinjiao (Sp-6) and Zhongfeng (Liv-4) is highly effective. Another approach is to place an intradermal needle in Sanyinjiao about a week before the start of menses to prevent the symptoms.

Prolapse of Uterus

Main Regimen:
Practice Inner Regulation Qigong with Hard Breathing. Initially practice in a lying posture and later use seated and standing postures. Concentrate on Dantian.

Complementary Exercise:
(1) Preventive Qigong: Back Rub, Dantian Rub, Leg Stretch
(2) Stepping Qigong: Striking Dantian

Pregnancy Toxemia

This condition includes symptoms in the late period of pregnancy such as edema, hypertension, and albuminuria (protein in urine).

Main Regimen:
Practice Vitalizing Qigong with Quiet Breathing. Alternate between the seated and standing postures. Concentrate on Dantian. Practice three to five times a day for thirty minutes to one hour at a time.

Complementary Exercise:
Relaxation Qigong: Two or three thirty-minute sessions a day

Note: Inner Regulation Qigong should not be practiced after the third month of pregnancy, and only natural breathing should be used when practicing Qigong.

Acupuncture:
In light cases, acupuncture can be effective against pregnancy toxemia. Nevertheless however, acupuncture is not recommended in the late stages of pregnancy and care must be taken not to let the stimulation become too strong. Generally, in order to avoid miscarriage, the abdominal area of a pregnant woman is seldom acupunctured. The points used for pregnancy toxemia are as follows: Xinhui (GV-22) on the head, Geshu (B-17), Pishu (B-20), and Weicang (B-50) on the back, Juque (CV-14) and Zhongwan (CV-12) in the upper abdomen, and Liangqiu (S-34) and Yanglingquan (G-34) on the legs.

Diseases of the Sense Organs

Glaucoma

Main Regimen:
Practice Relaxation Qigong in the reclining position. Practice up to five times a day for thirty minutes to an hour at a time.

Complementary Exercise:
(1)   Preventive Qigong: Eye Exercise, Face and Scalp Rub, Ear Exercise
(2)   Stepping Qigong

Acupuncture:
The symptom of pain in the eyes can be relieved through acupuncture. The most commonly used points include Zanzhu (B-2), Tianzhu (B-10), Tianliao (TE-15), Tongziliao (G-1), Shangguan (G-3), Xuanlu (G-5), Yangbai (G-14), Fengchi (G-20), and Jianjing (G-21).

Optic Atrophy

Main Regimen:
Practice Inner Regulation Qigong with Soft Breathing in any postures. Concentrate on Dantian.

Complementary Exercise:
(1)   Preventive Qigong: Eye Exercise, Face and Scalp Rub, Ear Exercise, Neck Exercise, Yongquan Massage
(2)   Tai Chi

Acupuncture:
Acupuncture can slow down the progress of this disease and it even partially restores eyesight in some cases. The points used are very similar to those listed for glaucoma.

Myopia

Follow the regimen and complementary exercises listed for optic atrophy.

Acupuncture:
For cases of. pseudomyopia, acupuncture can have a substantial effect and improve eyesight. The main points used are as follows: Tianzhu (B-10) and Fengchi (G-20) on the back of the neck; Ganshu (B-18), Tianliao (TE-15), and Jianjing (G-21) on the back; Zanzhu (B-2), Tongziliao (G-1), and Yangbai (G-14) around the eyes; Quchi (LI-11) on the arms; and Zhongfeng (Liv-4) on the ankels. In China, the "plum blossom needle" (a small hammer with little needles on the head that is tapped against the skin) is used to treat myopia in children. Generally the neck and shoulder region as well as the forehead are treated.

Central Retinitis

Follow the regimen and complementary exercises listed for optic atrophy. Acupuncture is effective and serves to relieve the symptoms.

Pigmentary Degeneration of Retina

Follow the regimen and complementary exercises listed for optic atrophy.

Chronic Tonsillitis

Main Regimen:
Practice Vitalizing Qigong with Quiet Breathing in the seated posture. Concentrate on Dantian.

Complementary Exercise:
Preventive Qigong: Tongue Exercise, Swallowing Saliva

Acupuncture:
Good results can be obtained with acupuncture. Acupuncturing Renying (S-9) is especially effective so this should be tried first. Otherwise, Tianzhu (B-10), Yifeng (TE-17), and Fengchi (G-20) on the neck, Dazhu (B-11) and Fengmen (B-12) on the upper back, Shufu (K-27) and Tiantu`(CV-22) on the upper chest, and Chize (L-5) and Hegu (LI-4) are commonly used points. Another approach used is to prick either Shaoshang (L-11) or Shaoze (SI-1) at the base of the fingernail and to squeeze out a drop or two of blood. Also, sometimes the area around the tonsils is punctured directly. Shallow insertion is sufficient in this case.

Nervous Deafness

Main Regimen:
Practice Inner Regulation Qigong with Hard Breathing, alternating between the lying and seated postures. Practice four to six times a day for thirty minutes to an hour at a time.

Complementary Exercise:
Stepping Qigong: Striking Dantian

Acupuncture:
Nervous deafness usually results from neurasthenia and other nervous disorders, and tinnitus often leads to hearing problems. Acupuncture can sometimes be effective. Mostly points around the ear as well as those in the neck and interscapular region are used. Relaxing the tension in the neck and shoulder area is often the key to improvement.

Menière's Disease

Main Regimen:
Practice Inner Regulation Qigong with Soft Breathing in the lying posture. Concentrate on Dantian. Practice four times a day for thirty minutes to an hour at a time.

Complementary Exercise:
(1) Vitalizing Qigong: Practice Quiet Breathing once in the morning and once at night.
(2) Preventive Qigong: Ear Exercise, Back Rub, Dantian Rub, Yongquan Massage

Acupuncture:

Good results can be obtained in relieving dizziness, but for cases involving laby-
rinthitis, the tinnitus and hearing problems are very difficult to cure. Generally, points
around the ear such as Yifeng (TE-17), Jiaosun (TE-20), Tinghui (G-2), and Wangu
(G-12) are used along with Baihui (GV-20), Tianzhu (B-10), and Zhengying (G-17)
on the head, Shenzhu (GV-12) and Fengmen (B-12) on the upper back, and Shaohai
(H-3) on the inside of the elbow. Also, on occasion, strong heat stimulation such as
moxibustion is used on Baihui.

Appendix: Diagrams of Acupuncture Points

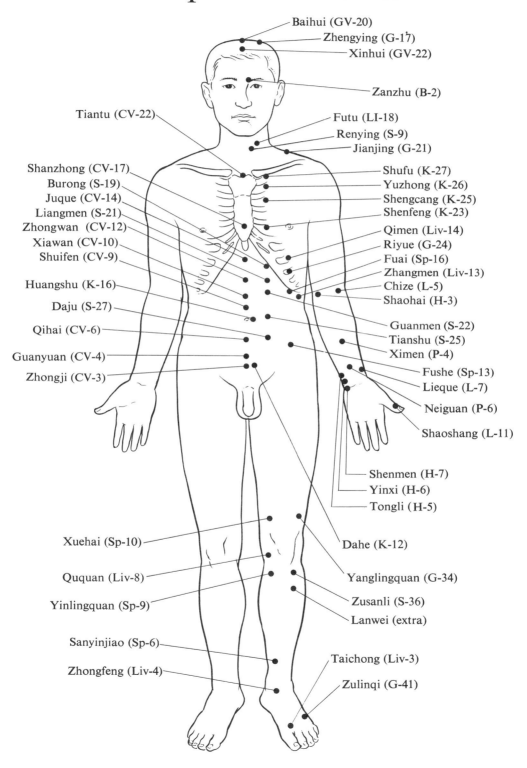

Baihui (GV-20)
Zhengying (G-17)
Xinhui (GV-22)

Zanzhu (B-2)

Tiantu (CV-22)

Futu (LI-18)
Renying (S-9)
Jianjing (G-21)

Shanzhong (CV-17)
Burong (S-19)
Juque (CV-14)
Liangmen (S-21)
Zhongwan (CV-12)
Xiawan (CV-10)
Shuifen (CV-9)

Huangshu (K-16)

Daju (S-27)

Qihai (CV-6)

Guanyuan (CV-4)

Zhongji (CV-3)

Shufu (K-27)
Yuzhong (K-26)
Shengcang (K-25)
Shenfeng (K-23)

Qimen (Liv-14)
Riyue (G-24)
Fuai (Sp-16)
Zhangmen (Liv-13)
Chize (L-5)
Shaohai (H-3)

Guanmen (S-22)
Tianshu (S-25)
Ximen (P-4)

Fushe (Sp-13)
Lieque (L-7)

Neiguan (P-6)

Shaoshang (L-11)

Shenmen (H-7)
Yinxi (H-6)
Tongli (H-5)

Xuehai (Sp-10)

Ququan (Liv-8)

Yinlingquan (Sp-9)

Sanyinjiao (Sp-6)

Zhongfeng (Liv-4)

Dahe (K-12)

Yanglingquan (G-34)

Zusanli (S-36)

Lanwei (extra)

Taichong (Liv-3)

Zulinqi (G-41)

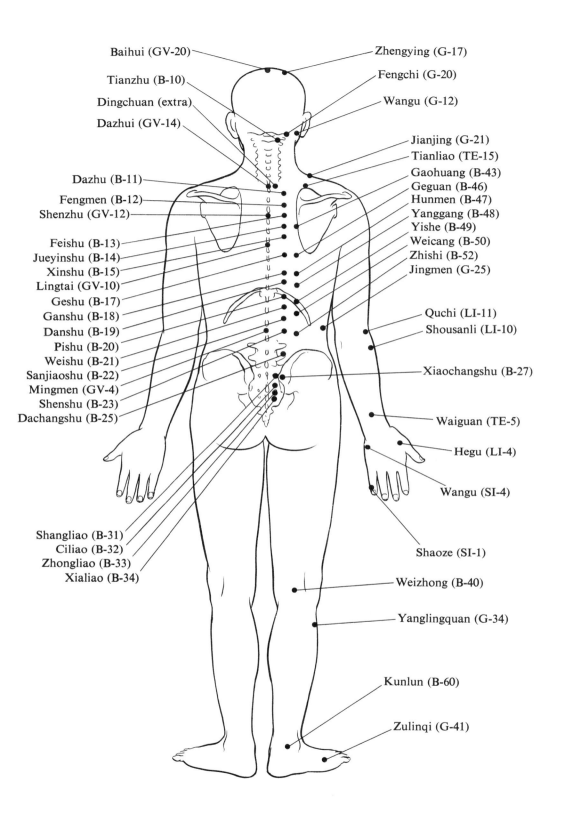

Baihui (GV-20)
Zhengying (G-17)
Tianzhu (B-10)
Fengchi (G-20)
Dingchuan (extra)
Wangu (G-12)
Dazhui (GV-14)
Jianjing (G-21)
Tianliao (TE-15)
Dazhu (B-11)
Gaohuang (B-43)
Fengmen (B-12)
Geguan (B-46)
Shenzhu (GV-12)
Hunmen (B-47)
Yanggang (B-48)
Yishe (B-49)
Feishu (B-13)
Weicang (B-50)
Jueyinshu (B-14)
Zhishi (B-52)
Xinshu (B-15)
Jingmen (G-25)
Lingtai (GV-10)
Geshu (B-17)
Ganshu (B-18)
Quchi (LI-11)
Danshu (B-19)
Shousanli (LI-10)
Pishu (B-20)
Weishu (B-21)
Sanjiaoshu (B-22)
Xiaochangshu (B-27)
Mingmen (GV-4)
Shenshu (B-23)
Dachangshu (B-25)
Waiguan (TE-5)
Hegu (LI-4)
Wangu (SI-4)
Shangliao (B-31)
Ciliao (B-32)
Zhongliao (B-33)
Xialiao (B-34)
Shaoze (SI-1)
Weizhong (B-40)
Yanglingquan (G-34)
Kunlun (B-60)
Zulinqi (G-41)

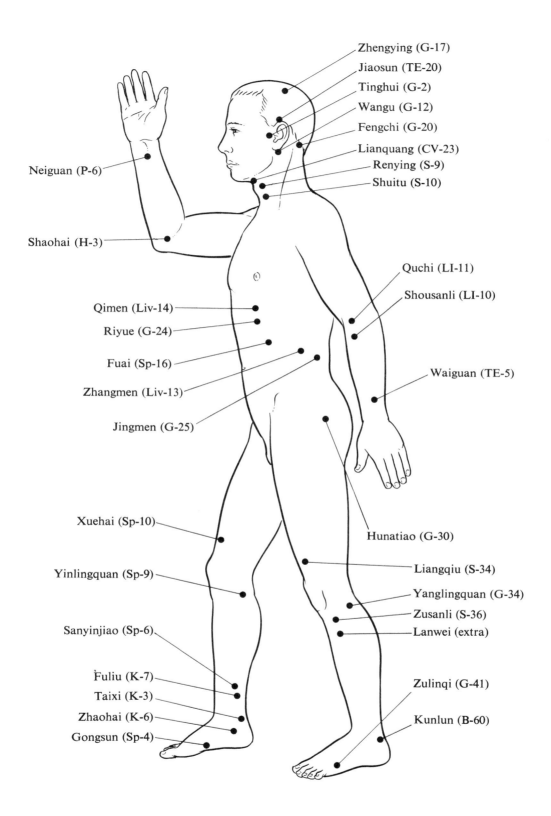

Zhengying (G-17)

Jiaosun (TE-20)

Tinghui (G-2)

Wangu (G-12)

Fengchi (G-20)

Lianquang (CV-23)

Renying (S-9)

Shuitu (S-10)

Neiguan (P-6)

Shaohai (H-3)

Quchi (LI-11)

Shousanli (LI-10)

Qimen (Liv-14)

Riyue (G-24)

Fuai (Sp-16)

Zhangmen (Liv-13)

Jingmen (G-25)

Waiguan (TE-5)

Xuehai (Sp-10)

Yinlingquan (Sp-9)

Sanyinjiao (Sp-6)

Fuliu (K-7)

Taixi (K-3)

Zhaohai (K-6)

Gongsun (Sp-4)

Hunatiao (G-30)

Liangqiu (S-34)

Yanglingquan (G-34)

Zusanli (S-36)

Lanwei (extra)

Zulinqi (G-41)

Kunlun (B-60)

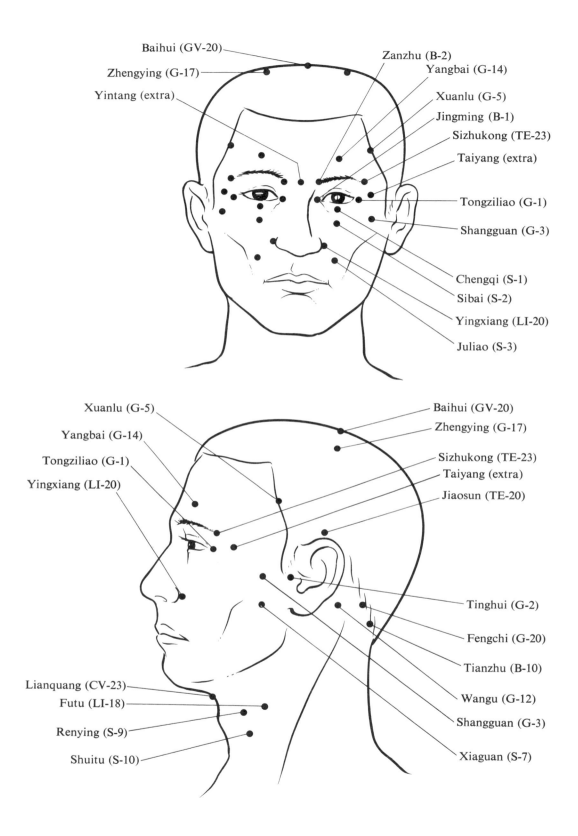

Baihui (GV-20)
Zhengying (G-17)
Yintang (extra)

Zanzhu (B-2)
Yangbai (G-14)
Xuanlu (G-5)
Jingming (B-1)
Sizhukong (TE-23)
Taiyang (extra)

Tongziliao (G-1)

Shangguan (G-3)

Chengqi (S-1)
Sibai (S-2)
Yingxiang (LI-20)
Juliao (S-3)

Xuanlu (G-5)
Yangbai (G-14)
Tongziliao (G-1)
Yingxiang (LI-20)

Baihui (GV-20)
Zhengying (G-17)
Sizhukong (TE-23)
Taiyang (extra)
Jiaosun (TE-20)

Tinghui (G-2)
Fengchi (G-20)
Tianzhu (B-10)
Wangu (G-12)
Shangguan (G-3)
Xiaguan (S-7)

Lianquang (CV-23)
Futu (LI-18)
Renying (S-9)
Shuitu (S-10)

Afterword

I first became interested in Oriental medicine because it emphasizes the natural healing powers in each individual. It only makes sense that the power which caused the miracle of life to come into being is capable of restoring a sick person to a healthy state. Also, I found Oriental medicine very appealing because it aims to detect and treat diseases at the earliest possible stage, even before there are any outward signs. Too many people today suffer unnecessarily because they fail to pay attention to the subtle signs of their body. And often, by the time an illness becomes manifested as a medical problem, a person has little choice other than to receive radical treatments involving drugs or surgery. I hoped that by practicing Oriental medicine I could play a small role in the growth of public awareness concerning the tremendous possibilities contained in self-healing.

This is how I came to enter the field of Oriental medicine, and it was the simple and natural thing for me to return to Japan, where I was born and raised, to take up the study of shiatsu and acupuncture. My interest in Oriental medicine increased as I learned more about it, but along with this a certain doubt began to grow within me. This was because the Oriental medicine I saw being practiced in Japan was not really so different from Western medicine. That is to say, many patients came to receive treatments from acupuncturists and left without gaining a better understanding about their own condition. I felt that Oriental medicine had to be more than just another health-care specialty. If the natural power of healing exists in every individual, it would seem most likely that the attitudes and actions of each individual count the most in activating this power. This belief caused me to begin looking into various practices for improving health including yoga and Zen meditation. These practices, I learned, were of definite value. Unfortunately, not too many people are inclined in these directions, perhaps in the belief that it requires some religious devotion. Furthermore, it is often difficult to get sick people to undertake such programs of exercise or meditation because the benefits are not so immediate or obvious.

Therefore, I was very excited when I first learned that in China exercise and meditation were being practiced on a massive scale in medical institutions with re-markable results. These practices were called Qigong, and it seemed to be a modern-ized version of Taoist exercises for health such as Do-In with the mystifying ele-ments removed except the focus on vital energy. Apparently there had been a move to outlaw such practices in China during a more extreme political climate, but controlled clinical tests·so clearly testified to the effectiveness of Qigong that it was given a special place in the Chinese health-care system. Qigong was just what I had been looking for.

My expectations were answered in China, where I saw patients in hospitals receiving instruction in Qigong. Also, I witnessed a great number of normal people in perfect health practicing Qigong exercises early in the morning. There was no doubt left in my mind that Qigong was going to become an important part of my practice in Oriental medicine. After returning to Japan, I sought someone to continue studying Qigong with and came across Dr. Takahashi's work on Qigong. He was very enthusiastic about spreading the practice of Qigong, and he immediately agreed when I suggested that we compile an English text on Dr. Liu's Qigong Therapy. Working together with Dr. Takahashi to produce this book has added greatly to my knowledge and practice of Qigong. Also, it has made me aware once again that all things worthwhile require time and consistent personal effort. I am very gratified that my dream of popularizing Qigong has begun to materialize in the form of this book. I remain committed to sharing this wisdom of the East to the rest of the world. I sincerely hope that every reader will put this knowledge to practical use for their own personal benefit to enjoy the best of health.

STEPHEN S. BROWN
N. I. A. O. M.
P.O. Box 31639
Seattle, WA. 98103

Index